In Praise of *The Art of Relationships*

An excellent beginning study of sexuality for the newly sexual. Jan's clarity is quite profound.

—**Dr. Pat Allen,** *Psychotherapist and nationally known author and lecturer*

Jan's book is a real page-turner as it takes you on an adventurous and often funny journey towards your discovery on how to create meaningful relationships.

—**Barbara Goutierre,** *Disney Brand Management*

This book has something special—something to do with Jan's no-bull, straightforward, tell-it-like-it-is, voice of reason and wisdom with a heart. It's like we've heard it all before but not like this.

—**Gail Kearns,** *Editor*

The Art of Relationships is for everyone …if you are ready to create happy and healthy relationships! You feel as if she's having a conversation with you as she leads you in developing your own style of creative togetherness.

—**Claire Elkins,** *Professor, Saddleback College*

The Art of Relationships is full of clear, practical, accessible advice that resonates with the wise voice of Jan Fritsen—author, teacher, therapist, coach and sage.

—**Dr. Melina Friedman,** *Associate Professor, Southern California College of Optometry*

In her book, *The Art of Relationships,* Ms. Fritsen has taken the classroom experience and recreated it into a textbook for life. It is not a read; it is a beautiful journey within self. It is also not a book to be shelved after completion; rather, it is a Bible for relationships that should be kept within hands' reach and revisited on a regular basis. This book can be opened to any page, and Ms. Fritsen's words and down-to-earth insights will take the reader where he or she needs to go.

—**Carrie Lynn Moore,** *Teacher & Artist.* ⌐ *Healing Heart Seminars*

Whether you're a single person looking to bu¹ⁱ lasti   hed couple continuing to grow together, or a⌐ strengthen friendships and family t¹   ⌐ⅰⅰspire you to succeed with deeper understandⅰ

—**Holland Carney**   *⌐ⅰinking Group*

I often have hoped for an outline or blue   ⌐are with my clients so that they would have a guideline for building h⌐ ⌐ny, loving relationships. Jan Fritsen has created a wonderful workbook that I would recommend to all my clients before they embark on their next relationship. I believe by using this book, they can avoid past mistakes and find the type of relationship that we all long for.

— **Roe Piccoli,** *Family Therapist, Director of The Center for Family Healing*

Jan Fritsen has created a work of art... a clear and precise format to healthy relationships. Her expertise spells it out in a straightforward language as to how we experience human relationships from infancy to adulthood. Her "action items" give the reader the opportunity to recreate what was not given to them in their childhood, to have and achieve what they desire now in their adult relationships. This book will change how you experience relationships — for the better.

— **Dr. M.P. Wylie, Author of** *Journey to Love: Attracting & Building Loving Relationships*

This book is excellent for anyone considering a new relationship or beginning a new relationship and especially for college students and young people at various stages of their relationships. It would make an excellent text for a college class but is also good reading for an individual outside the classroom. I was especially impressed with the way Jan made complicated psychodynamic concepts vivid, accessible, lively and understandable.

— **Vivian Clecak, M.S.W., L.C.S.W., M.F.T.,** *Executive Director of Human Options, a women's shelter*

Jan's years of experience as a teacher, clinician and counselor are evident throughout this creative work. She addresses complex topics and provides workable strategies for a variety of relationship issues.

— **Mindy Bingham,** *Author and Publisher, Academic Innovations*

I remember someone once saying, "If only I'd known then what I know now..." What if we took that chance to know now? This is the moment when the lights come on and we get that delicious opportunity to "get it". The river of life is easier to navigate when someone hands you the oar that has been at your feet all the time and teaches you how to row. Don't read this book once. Read it twice. Share the journey. That's what you wanted to do in the first place, anyway!

— **Margi Murray, M.A, M.S., RPC**

Jan has taken her experience as a counselor, coach, professor and artist in this well written, enlightening and educational book to show clearly how relationships can become magnificent journeys and not something you cling to in order to survive!

— **Sholeh Alizadeh, Ph.D.,** *Director of the Re-Entry/Women's Center, Saddleback College, CA*

The Art of Relationships

The Art of Relationships

How to create togetherness that works

Jan Fritsen

Insightful Publishing
Laguna Beach, California

The Art of Relationships
How to Create Togetherness That Works

by Jan Fritsen

Published by:

Insightful Publishing
303 Broadway, Suite 104-19
Laguna Beach, California 92651
www.insightfulpublishing.com

Publisher's Cataloging-In-Publication Data
(Prepared by The Donohue Group, Inc.)

Fritsen, Jan.
   The art of relationships : how to create togetherness that works / Jan Fritsen.
      p. : ill. ; cm.
   Includes bibliographical references.
   ISBN-13: 978-0-9773937-0-1
   ISBN-10: 0-9773937-0-4
   1. Man-woman relationships. 2. Interpersonal relations.
   3. Intimacy (Psychology) 4. Couples. 5. Love. I. Title.
   HQ801 .F75 2006
   306.7

Cover Design by Peri Poloni, Knockout Design, Placerville, California
www.knockoutbooks.com
Interior Design by Christine Nolt, Cirrus Design, Santa Barbara, California
Cartoons by Allen Loman, Laguna Beach, California
Edited by Gail M. Kearns, To Press and Beyond, Santa Barbara, California
www.topressandbeyond.com

Printed in the United States of America

Dedicated to you, the reader, for seeking

self understanding and making healthy relationships

a priority in your life.

And to my students, who insisted that I write this book.

College students gave their teacher the assignment to write a book about what she taught them that changed their lives. This is the result. Follow their favorite lessons through the student-driven curriculum which led to fascinating discussions and some surprising insights.

Contents

Warning-disclaimer

This book is designed to provide information on relationships. It is written and sold with the understanding that the publisher and author are not engaged in rendering professional counseling services via the printed page. You may find this book therapeutic but it is not a substitute for therapy. Relationships are a "do it yourself journey". The author is on this journey too. If you are having problems emotionally or are in a high risk relationship, use this book as a starting point but please follow up with a professional therapist.

Dear Reader,

What can this book possibly give you that adds to all the other self help books you've read?

Relationships enhance, modify, change us, make us grow and, sometimes, drive us crazy. Relationships mentor us, so choosing the right people for the right reasons will help us to be sane.

You have picked up this book because you are interested in relationships, because you have one and are proud of it, because you want one and don't have one, because you had one and it ended and you want to get a new one or because you are intrigued with the idea of relationships, period.

Relationships are something you do! They are important, and you want people in your life that will be nourishing to you and to whom you can give away that storehouse of love you have been saving up.

And you want to know how to do some things better than you did in the last relationship.

This book gives you some strategies that you can think about and use — today. Try a few chapters.

You don't need to read the entire book to begin creating the togetherness you want! Read the chapters that speak to you right now. While the book builds information chapter by chapter, each chapter stands alone if you want to skim or be selective.

I wrote this book for you. I hope it helps.

Some Opening Thoughts . . .

I stopped by to visit a family recently. One child was engrossed in video games. One kid was playing back the answering machine for messages and leaving a text message for another machine. Father was online on the computer. Mother was listening to headphones. The TV was blaring. The aunt was reading the paper. A teen was doing an exercise video. The uncle was playing laptop solitaire.

The pets were sleeping and I, I was looking for a little human interaction. Instead, there was isolation and insulation.

What kind of humans are we growing today? I can work at home, order everything by fax, e-mail or online. There is distance learning by computer or TV. I can date by computer, go to a chat room online, watch movies on my TV by dialing a computer and ordering it. There is even safe sex (so to speak) by computer. Virtual reality can trick my brain into any almost real experience. And when I am depressed because of feeling alienated and alone, my doctor will quickly prescribe an antidepressant.

According to the newspaper, more than 50 percent of the population now take antidepressants. Even children are being given antidepressants. If our country is so much in need of antidepressants to combat depression, perhaps we should look at the prevention of depression instead of medicating it.

Alcohol is wreaking havoc on our families. It alienates people from each other. It is the most dangerous drug around when you count auto accidents, treatment programs, death from liver disease and the emotional costs families face that live with an alcoholic. Twelve-step programs abound to help people cope with addictions galore. From video games to twelve-step programs—all of this is designed to help us feel less alone.

What I hear from people more and more is: I do not feel held by anyone or anything. I do not feel connected to anyone or any group. I feel lonely, even when I am with other people, and sometimes even with my mate. I hardly know who I am because there is so much change all around me and in my life.

Creating and maintaining togetherness requires that we have a vision of what we want to create followed by the hard work of putting our skills and talents to use. With all the knowledge we can gather and the resources available to us, we can bring our relationship vision to life. This is art. This is what we explore together in this book.

Together we will be dealing with matters of consequence. We will be dealing with your need to be a connected human being, to understand and to be able to navigate human relationships of all kinds.

You will embark on the most important space exploration there is today. You'll explore inner space — what a relationship feels like from the inside. You will explore the space between us. You will explore what it is to have relationships and to love. Most of all, you will explore you!

I just want to know where this relationship is going.

I don't know. Maybe out to dinner or something.

14

Chapter 1

What Are Relationships For?

"Assumptions are the termites of relationships."

— Henry Winkler

How is it that when two people say they want to have a relationship with each other, that there are so many misunderstandings about what that means? Defining the words we use to talk about relationships may help you get what you really want. Drawing a map of your relationship history may give you a pictorial means of looking at the impact of the people in your life on your life.

Who doesn't want to have a relationship? Most people eagerly seek a partner or special friend or mate. In fact, most make the finding of a significant other a priority in their lives. However, few people bother to define what a relationship actually is and assume that the other person's definition is the same as theirs. When you say you want a relationship, what specifically do you want?

ACTION ITEM ··········▶

Getting Specific

To get started, ask yourself these three questions:

1. What are you looking for in a relationship? (friendship, companionship, intimacy, etc.?)

2. Who do you want in this relationship with you? (traits, gender, age, etc.)

3. What is the purpose of this relationship? (dating, sex, marriage, financial benefits, etc.?)

Write down as many answers as you can think of. Then review your list. Is this what you really want? The range and variety of answers to these questions are endless. You can do this for a current relationship or to look at what was missing in a past relationship.

As you think about these questions, begin a journal. In it, you can jot down your thoughts as you read this book and include your insights and reactions to the ACTION ITEMS as you complete them.

Here are some responses to the questions that other people have given.

What are you looking for?

Sharing, emotional connection, caring for one another, trusting, good communication, bonding, exchange of energy, respecting, commitment, love.

Who do you want in this relationship?

Family, friends, significant others, someone my own age, someone older than me to take care of me, God, nature, people, people with similar interests or values.

Sometimes we find our relationships to be not with people but with our work, our art, our pets or even our computer, bikes, cars, books, music.

What is the purpose of this relationship?

Fulfillment, to share feelings, to learn, to feel safe, companionship, to get love/be loved, to feel needed, to know they are there, to learn about self, to get my mother off my back, to create my own family, so I'm not alone, mutual benefit, growth, joy, security, sex, to enjoy life, to be accepted, to have fun.

What answers did you come up with?

Hold on to what you have written. You can add or delete as you go along. We will come back to these notes later. Your particular answers may reflect a wide variety of connections. You are unique. Your list is unique and everyone else's list has the potential of being uniquely different from yours.

Take a moment to go back to prioritize your lists for each of the three questions. What description is at the top of each list for you?

Select the top answer to each of the three questions and put the three together in a sentence to determine your personal definition of the kind of relationship you desire.

For example:

1. I want a commitment
2. with a significant other
3. to enjoy life together.

This definition, or something like it, is a starting place for what you want in a relationship or what your expectations are when searching for a special other.

At a particular point, you might ask someone if they want to have a relationship with you. If they say yes, you still won't know what they are agreeing to until you ask them to define the three areas above and compare them with your definition. You could be agreeing to something you might not really want!

Consider This

What if your definition of a relationship is: I want an emotional connection with a significant other for fulfillment, spiritual growth and love?

But you become involved with someone whose definition is: I want to hang out and hook up with people at a sex club for purposes of excitement and sex?

You both use the same word — relationship — but you have entirely different ideas about what that word means. What conflicts might arise for a couple with these two lists? The only way to know what the other person is thinking or expecting, is to talk to them about it, listen carefully to what they have to say. . . and then talk some more!

How would the relationship definition be different for:

- Teen age boys?
- College women?
- Previously married persons?
- Male groups?
- Female groups?
- Senior citizens?

Take a few minutes to jot down a few definitions you think would fit for each group. How do they compare with yours?

Always start with what you *really* want!

Sometimes, as we age, there is a sense of urgency about potential relationships in our lives. We ask ourselves questions like:

▶ "Whom will I have lunch with?" (This can be a major concern when in high school.)
▶ "When will I meet Mr. or Ms. Right?"
▶ "How will I know if the person I'm seeing is the right one for me?"
▶ "What do I want from the person I'm seeing? How do I know for sure that this is what I really want?"
▶ "Who am I now?" after a relationship has ended.

Relationships teach us to value ourselves. It is not about *finding* the right person but about *becoming* the right person. My friend Ginny describes it as discovering what is true for us about ourselves and then becoming the best of that truth that we can be.

We have sex education in the schools, but there is no such

thing as relationship education in school curriculums. I think early relationship education is as essential as sex education.

How we value ourselves, along with wanting to be in a relationship, is what drives us—into good and bad choices. It has to be both because "wanting a relationship" without "valuing ourselves" will never lead to good choices, only bad ones. When we do value ourselves and our personal definition of what we really want in a relationship, we are more capable of making good choices.

ACTION ITEM ··········▶

Mapping Your Relationships

Take the time now to draw maps of relational connections that you've experienced so far in your life. When you finish them, keep your maps with your book so you can use them in later chapters. **Examples of relationship maps and a guide to symbols can be seen on pages 308–312.**

How to Do It

Think about the people in your life who are significant enough to be on your mind or who are involved with you right now.

Drawing Your Maps—Step by Step

1. Draw your map on a page or half-page sheet of blank paper.

2. Put yourself in the middle by drawing a circle and labeling it with your name.

3. Draw circles to represent the people who are in your life by placing them near or distant from your circle and label who these persons are. These will be people that you think about, who add energy to your life or take energy from it. They are significant to your development or history. Yes, pets fit on this map if you wish.

4. If it's a group like the soccer team or church or neighborhood group, draw a circle with circles inside it to indicate a group.

5. If it is a person who has passed away, draw your circle with a dotted line. If it's a person not personally known to you but a mentor or hero, the dotted line applies here too.

After this first map is completed, look back in time and do maps in five-year intervals. While five-year intervals seem to work best, there may be some years that were just too special to skip, so you can be flexible in your time zones.

For example, do maps for ages 5, 10, 15, 20, 25 and 30 etc. Are you chronologically gifted? You may create many more maps if you wish! For your teen years, you might want to do maps for ages 16, 17 and 18 separately because so much was happening to you then. If you had a couple of years along the way that you'd like to emphasize, go ahead and make separate maps for them. There is no limit to the number of maps you may create.

These are your personal maps. You may design them anyway you want to. You can make them into an art project or simply sketch them out with circles and labels. Do what suits you best. It doesn't matter if they're beautiful. They don't have to be perfect. They just need to be functional for you personally.

You don't need to list neighbors or relatives if they were not special to you in some way. The maps are also "living entities" because you can add to them as we go through the chapters or remove people if you decide that you feel differently about them at some point. One young woman completed her maps and then exclaimed, "Gosh, I forgot my husband!"

As you complete each chapter, you'll be able to refer back to your maps and label the persons if the content applies to them (i.e., a holding person, an attachment person, a validating person).

You may find that some of the things that come up for you are pleasant, and some not so pleasant. As you notice the feelings that come up for you, try not to judge them but just notice them and say to yourself, isn't that interesting? Add your feelings to your journal.

As you create these maps in five-year intervals you'll begin to see a pattern of people who were a part of your life and may or may not be now. Maybe they were in your life in a significant way and then gone, replaced by someone else.

Each map charts the people who were or are in your life. Isn't it interesting to watch as they weave in and out of your life over time?

The maps reflect where you have come from and the people who have been part of your history. The art of relationships begins with looking at what works, what hurts, and what you can do to create the togetherness that you want.

(At the end of each chapter, the bulletin board will be filled with student and client comments and observations—reactions to the chapter. If you wish, you can write down your own observations in your journal.)

Relationships change... Just when you get comfortable with a situation, it's likely to change, but knowing that ahead of time makes it so much easier when the change comes.... By getting through the rough parts, I can look forward to happiness. (Martha, 37)

> At this phase of my life I'm moving forward on a different level. Looking at myself. Forgiving myself. Picturing a future of life. That's pretty scary. It's time to take responsibility for my life—no more closing my eyes or looking away, pretending. It's time to figure out how to garden and till the soil here and cause my life to be beautiful. (Diana, 50)

A relationship is something to learn and grow from. Sharing experiences with others, be it sailing around the world or simply sipping a cup of tea, is what makes us who we are. We build ourselves with the people we know, for it would not be possible alone. (Zack, 23)

> When I was drawing the maps, I noticed that I felt happiest when I had the most number of circles close to me, ages 5 to 10 and 35 to 40. I also noticed I felt sad that I didn't feel closer to my family and relatives. There was a pattern in all my age groups to have only a few close friends. I've not allowed many people into my life and have been pretty much a loner. Also, my friends at a younger age were ones that I did things with; they were not ones that I confided in, as I do now. (Tina, 40)

My father has always held, validated and protected me. I thought for a long time that he wasn't proud of me because he would never look at me when he talked. Then one day, I realized that's who he is and he will never desert me, cause me harm or let me think small. He shows his love in so many other ways. (Diana, 50)

Thanks to the loving, caring and supportive family relationships I was blessed with, I am the result of a wonderful creation accomplished by team work! (Marilyn, 21)

As I was creating my relationship maps, I noticed that once someone was in my life, they were in it forever. Losing attachments is definitely the hardest thing for me. (Maxine, 41)

What Are Relationships For?

Boy is he gonna be good looking when he gets a car!

Chapter 2

The Hype of "My Type"

"Personally, I like two types of men — domestic and foreign."
                                                    — Mae West

In our dating and friendship language, we refer to others as being our type, or not our type. When we walk into a room full of strangers, we usually identify someone or a particular group with which we want to connect. Why do we do that? And do we exclude meaningful others because of a familiar habit or a rush to judgment?

25

I am always delighted when students and my private practice clients tell me they are excited to be dating someone who they say is not their previous type! I am delighted because it means they have gotten past stereotypes in choosing the people they wish to spend time with and might be choosing more wisely.

Perhaps the question behind this chapter is, "Why do you keep selecting the people you do?" (Particularly if these folks do not seem to meet your needs!) "Gary, Larry and Harry" all seemed so different at first and wound up being the same as the last guy or gal—(Mary, Sherry or Carrie). Have you experienced this?

What Is "My Type?"

The simplest explanation of type is that it is about connecting and being comfortable with characteristics familiar to us.

- Everyone has a type.
- Everyone knows exactly what it is.
- You know who you are attracted to!

Can you describe in great detail the type of person you are attracted to or are searching for? When you walk into a room full of strangers, do you notice you are drawn to a certain type of person that just seems comfortable to be with? If the type of person you are attracted to is delightful and meets your needs, congratulations! If, however, being with your type causes you sadness or harm, it's important to read further.

Despite the clarity of one's response to type, type operates below our radar and tends to lead us around by the nose. We repeat the experiences that we don't want to repeat, time and time again. Every person we date or marry disappoints us.

My favorite example is of a woman who had been married five times and divorced five times because all her husbands were alcoholics. She announced that she had fallen in love again and was getting married to a wonderful guy.

In unison, her friends asked her, "Where did you meet him?" and her response was (you guessed it), "in a bar"!

So what is it that "type" can teach us so that we benefit from our mistakes and don't need to learn the same lesson over and over?

Typical Type Scenarios

We respond to certain characteristics in a person because the familiarity makes us comfortable with him or her. We recognize patterns and know how to act with people who behave in a way that feels familiar to us. We feel comfortable even when the behavior may be unpleasant because we know what to expect from it and think we can handle it. Perhaps we could even call it habit.

Along comes someone who looks great on the outside. You think he is different at first blush, but there's something about him that's familiar. Perhaps this person looks like the last one you were with. She has a certain look that's attractive to you. One young man referred to his type as a "tight package" and the succession of his girlfriends looked pretty much alike.

"Gary, Larry and Harry" all seemed different at first and yet they wound up being repeats of previous experiences.

Then there's the dilemma of the "nice guy."

Many women say they just want to have a nice guy in their lives and, yet, they consistently are attracted to a more exciting guy (their type) and find out that the excitement brings exactly what they don't want.

On the flip side, this is why nice guys are frustrated. They know they are nice guys (sweet, honest, kind and attentive, etc.) and yet they consistently lose the woman to a not so nice guy who may treat her poorly. So the cycle continues because women want nice (they really do) and yet choose what they consider to be "exciting," which translates as a problem type from habit and recognition of familiar behavior.

One woman stated that she really did want a nice guy but didn't wish to be with a boring guy. She equated a nice guy with boring. As she and I talked further, it became clear what she really wanted and she saw that she didn't have to give up the exciting part to be with a nice guy. What she had to give up was the abusive behaviors that seemed to go with her familiar exciting type, and reframe her thinking.

This goes both ways of course. The "nice woman" isn't as exciting to the man as the slightly crazy woman he seems drawn to and then disappointed by, time after time.

Are you wanting to be with a nice guy or gal and yet sending the message to them to stay away?

Our type usually recognizes us too. We send, as well as receive, subtle signals to approach or to keep some distance. This is the beginning of who we allow into our circle. If we want to expand our circle, we need to put out the welcome sign. If we want to change the circle, we need to change who we show the welcome sign to.

Rather than the journey of continued damage, it becomes helpful to make some conscious rather than unconscious choices. Consciousness means reacting to a *shopping list* rather than reacting to *impulse* or *habit* choices.

What is familiar will always show up first. To look beyond the habit will take consciously changing your focus.

The first step is to make a list of what you want in a mate or friend or partner. Yes, a list may sound cold or calculating, but would you go shopping for a car without having the characteristics and features that you want clearly in mind?

You would most likely shop for a particular style, color, certain features and at least a solid engine with working parts. You may also gravitate to a certain make and year of cars and would not consider other makes and models at all.

One should at least be as particular about a selecting a mate as one is about selecting a car!

ACTION ITEM ··········►

The Shopping List

1. Make your own detailed shopping list now. As you make your list, be sure to include ALL the characteristics you want, including both major and minor ones. The more detailed the list is, the clearer you will be about the desired person. You deserve the best person for you!

   It's okay to be choosy. After all, you'll be spending lots of time with this person and sharing time, finances, health, energy, relatives, social events, and perhaps children, beliefs, politics and probably sex.

   Some sample ideas from other people's lists are: sense of humor, spiritual, compassionate, playful, attractive, honest, fun to be with, good conversationalist, unselfish, likes the outdoors, good with money, interested in having a family, nonsmoker, adventurous, good figure, a morning person, good values, sensitive, and more.

A seventy-year-old added to her brainstormed list that she would like him to be well endowed!

2. Review your list to see what might be missing. Where do you list love, trustworthy and kindness? Some people forget to include them on their list! Isn't that interesting?

   Making assumptions and neglecting to name exactly what you want could lead to finding a person that you don't want, or someone with totally different values than you desire.

3. Next, rate your top three or four characteristics. These differ from person to person. Take a moment to prioritize your list from most important to least important.

   - If you are with someone, how closely does your list describe them?
   - How does your list compare to the type of person you usually date or spend time with?
   - Are you actually attracted to people with the characteristics on your list? (or do you list them because you think you should?) If there is a difference between your list and your reality, then no wonder you're not satisfied or happy with your relationship!

   If your list is a completely different prioritized list from any list your partner would make, no wonder there is conflict in your relationship!

4. Once you have your list, use it. Refer back to it frequently.

While making your list, be firm with yourself. If someone doesn't meet your criteria, don't spend time with them. Any time or energy spent with the *wrong* one will keep you from meeting the *right* one.

Your prioritized list includes items of greater and lesser importance. Are the important characteristics you desire present in the person you are now seeing? There are perhaps some minor items that can be trade-offs but major non-negotiable items are essential. If you don't hold out for them, they will become heart breakers. What are your non-negotiable items?

The Big But

When you call your best friend and start talking to her about your connection to a new friend, do you say things like, "he is everything on my list!"?

Do you find yourself enumerating every quality you wanted?

If you have this conversation with your friend and at the end of it add the word BUT, listen carefully to what you say after that. Remember, BUT cancels out everything that came before it, no matter how good the list is.

- But he's already married!
- But she killed her last boyfriend!
- But he served time in prison!
- But she's an alcoholic!
- But he isn't interested in a monogamous relationship!
- But she has been divorced three times!
- But he's supporting fourteen children from previous relationships! (At least he's responsible!)

These kinds of BUTS are deal-breakers despite the long list of other incredibly positive characteristics.

ACTION ITEM ·········➤

What is your list of deal-breakers?

If, when your friend asks at the end of the long list, "What is the BUT?" and you can honestly reply, "There is no but," then you have someone worth spending time with. Go for it!

As you become better acquainted, check your list frequently. Usually when we first start dating a person, both persons are on their best behavior. After a month or so, both people start relaxing together and becoming more themselves and it's as if two different people show up! Does that sound familiar to you?

So, as you become acquainted, remember to go back to your original list, just to check on what you really want! As you review your list, you may be pleasantly surprised to find there is a good fit with the person. It is particularly satisfying when your list and someone else's list are complementary. In fact, this is how togetherness that works, works.

Re-evaluating or questioning your type becomes a guide to understanding your patterns and relationship history as well as a guideline to a better connection with other people that you want in your life.

The Hype of "My Type"
Bulletin Board

I no longer will be looking for my type. My type has surely been an awful one. For too long I have tried to make people happy and tried to solve problems, always resulting with me right smack in the middle of one. It no longer will be my habit, but rather I will make my new habit one in which I am selective and cautious. I will take my time to grow into attachment and love and ask myself, "Are there any BUTS that I'm missing here?" (Karen, 25)

I was attracted to the bad boys. They seemed sexy and dangerous. I have learned that if I want to be nurtured and loved, maybe the bad boys aren't such a good choice. (Kristen, 21)

I think the reason I have not met Mr. Right yet is because I'm so damn picky. And that's a great thing. (Wendy, 33)

My type template was molded for a loser. I always seemed to want a bad boy so I could turn him around and make him a good boy. I have come to realize that I was totally wrong and should be looking for a good man. (Trudy, 29)

I hung out with people that put me down and criticized me, because my brothers had always done that to me. I figured others did that if they cared, and at least they paid attention to me in some way. I started getting so depressed from the confusion, and the emotional, mental and physical abuse from my friends and/or boyfriends, without the help of my family, that I became anorexic. (Carla, 18)

It took my breath away when I looked at my list and saw that Mike was everything I wanted in a life partner, even if he was so *not* my type. I was stunned. It was true that he was what I really wanted. Years later, he remains the love of my life. Wow. (Noreen, 55)

Two things that I do NOT want in a woman: overly religious or an alcoholic. (Adam, 21)

When I'm really interested in someone, it's hard for me to relax and just be myself. Still, I know that I'm most attractive when I'm being myself. (Frances, 19)

"There are two types of people — those who come into a room and say, 'well, here I am!' and those who come in and say, 'Ah, there you are.'"

— Frederick L. Collins

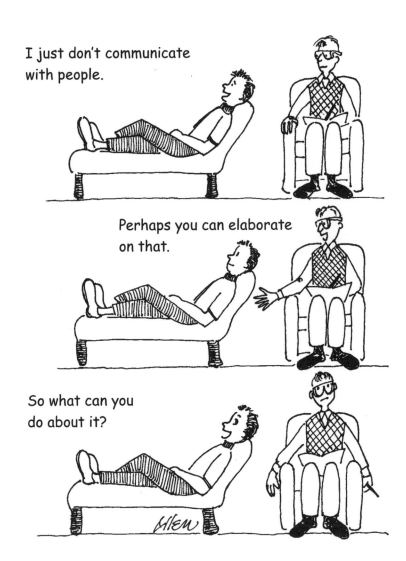

Chapter 3

The Wanting Disorder

"Unless someone truly has the power to say no, they never truly have the power to say yes."

— Dan Millman

Behind the words I don't know *is a possible disorder, which is illuminated in this chapter. The insight shared here offers a ready cure for the habit.*

There are many disorders in the world: eating disorders, behavior disorders and character disorders, to name a few. I would like to suggest there might also be a wanting disorder.

It can begin in childhood.

It may have started one night, at bedtime. A child says, "I want a drink of water." Mother replies, "You don't want that." The child responds, "Yes, I do, I want a drink of water." Mother says, "You don't want that."

This can lead to confusion because the child is thirsty and wants a drink of water, but the mother or father who is older and wiser, bigger and stronger, says, "You don't want that." So the child thinks to himself, okay, I guess I don't want that.

Why might the mother or the father say, "You don't want that?" Maybe they don't want to have to get up and take the child to the bathroom, they don't want the child to wet the bed or they suspect the child is stalling, trying to stay up longer. Maybe the child just had a drink, or it's late, it's time to go to sleep. Perhaps they want to avoid going all the way downstairs to get it. Mom's too tired, Dad's too tired. All of these concerns go through the minds of the parents.

The child simply said, "I'm thirsty, I want a drink of water." And for all of these reasons that the child doesn't understand, the parent replies, "You don't want that."

So, either the child wants it more, or gets confused. She is, after all, thirsty. There is a total disconnect between the child's request and the parent's response.

Does consistently giving a child what the child wants avoid the wanting disorder? No way! I don't mean to imply that children should have everything they want. Common sense says we must at times say no.

How does a parent say NO without saying "You don't want that."

Explanations help; tell them *why* in simple terms they can understand. If a child is told she cannot have a drink of water because there is no water or that she will have to wait, she can accept that. If a parent says, "I'll give you a half glass of water because I don't want you to have to get up in the middle of the night to go to the bathroom," then she can accept that, too.

A bit older, in the supermarket, the child says, "I want an ice cream." Mom says, "You don't want that." "Yes, I do." "No, you don't." Her reasons might be logical; the child will spoil his appetite for dinner, the ice cream has too much sugar, or it's not healthy, or it's just not convenient. But all she says is, "You don't want that."

Telling a child, "you don't want that" announces that not only is the request denied but also the feeling of wanting is being disallowed. One person is making a decision regarding another person's wants. It tends to be a *habit* answer rather than a *make sense* answer.

Here's the pattern: You tell someone that you want something, and someone else overrides your desire, telling you "you don't want that." There is a consistent theme; you say *I want* and they say *you don't want.*

When a two-year-old says, "I want a cookie," he knows precisely what he wants. If you hesitate to give it, he repeats, "I WANT A COOKIE AND I WANT IT RIGHT NOW." He will have a tantrum until you give him that cookie; he is extremely focused.

What happens to us as we age is that we begin to listen to voices saying, "YOU DON'T WANT THAT."

How often do you look at the dessert tray at the end of a meal in a restaurant and you know you want something? You are trying to choose between death by chocolate and key lime pie when someone says, "No, you don't want any." You really do want one of those desserts but the comment may bring enough intimidation with it so that you respond, "Never mind, I guess I don't want anything."

"When I grow up I want to be a fireman, an artist, etc." "YOU DON'T WANT THAT." You bring home a boyfriend, a girlfriend, a pair of shoes or a new car, and Mom or Dad says, "You don't want that." You hear this over and over again.

When you express what it is that you really want, you are risking yourself, and not being understood is tremendously painful.

You try to explain to a person something that's really important to you, like "this is what I want to do with my life" and they don't understand. Ouch! "This is something I want to achieve" or "this is who I think I am" and they don't understand. Ouch! If they are an important person to you, and they don't understand, you may give up and wilt inside.

After a while, when someone says to you, "What do you want?" how do you answer? You finally figure out that the safe answer is "I don't know." This is the **crux** of the wanting disorder. So you've switched from saying, "I want this" to "I don't know." It has become unsafe to say *I want*. You are rebuked. You express your opinion and someone, particularly an important someone, does not validate it. What you want is not valid.

You used to know what you wanted, but you learned to play it safe. You don't want to risk disapproval. You don't want to hear someone say, "You don't want that." Depending on how strong this message is over time, there comes a point when you are asked: "What do you want?" And how do you answer them? "I don't know." If they press it more, you say, "I should want" or "I ought to want" or "Whatever you want" or "Whatever anyone else wants" or "Whatever is best."

You begin to protect yourself by saying, "I don't know"... and you don't.

You answer this way because it's too much of a risk to take a position. At the point where you no longer know what you want, or you become afraid to express what you want, you have moved into a wanting disorder.

The wanting disorder is when you are afraid to express what you want; possibly for fear of disapproval, or out of habit, where you no longer are willing to take the chance of expressing an opinion or a *want*. You are shutting down. If you are in the habit of saying, "I don't know," it becomes easier to say that than to express what you want.

ACTION ITEM

Gaining Insight

Think about the following questions:

▶ What role has the phrase "You don't want that" played in your life?

▶ When did someone tell you "You don't want that?"

▶ Who were they?

▶ Can you remember what it was that you wanted?

▶ Conversely, have you ever told someone they didn't want what they said they wanted?

Does reading this give you any insight into what might have been going on? Write your thoughts in your journal.

If You Did Know

In my office, I'll sometimes ask a client what they would like to be, or to do, or to major in or what they really want. Many times they'll say they don't know. I'll follow up with, "Well, what if you DID know?" Then they say, "Oh, I'd like to be a bookkeeper or a fireman, or a doctor, or be married or single or travel."

By posing the question, "Well, what if you did know?" they come up with a quick answer. This is a little trick I have learned. You can use it. When you ask someone a question and they answer they don't know, follow up with "Well, what if you did know?" and wait for their answer. It will come!

One of the things that happens with this wanting disorder is that we begin to avoid the confrontation altogether. The other thing we might do is to shift our strategy. Most of us can get very clever about this. We start responding with what we don't want instead of talking about what we DO want.

The Power of Veto

How does the power of veto work? It's like this: I know what I want. I don't want to make a choice. I make you take the risk while I keep the power of veto. I keep saying no until you suggest whatever it is I wanted in the first place. It's a game.

If you are a person with this disorder, when a friend suggests, "Let's go out to eat" and asks where you want to go, you might say, "I don't know—I don't care." They begin to suggest Mexican food or Sushi, Chinese food or such and such a restaurant. You greet each possibility on the list with "No I don't want that." Finally, they mention a restaurant where you wanted to go all along and you say, "Okay."

What you learn with the wanting disorder is the power of veto. What you have learned is that it's much safer to veto someone else's choice than it is to start with "This is what I want." It has something to do with the habit of being taught very early on that when you express what you want, you not only don't get what you want, you are also put down for expressing what you want.

There are other times when you are simply indecisive and looking for something to tilt the decision. There are also times when you truly don't know—for example, what is the square root of 9,000,006, and you say you don't know. That's a fair answer. But "what are you hungry for?" "I don't know?" Of course you know. Sometimes it's just too risky to put it out there and say *I want* because of the *learned fear* that someone is going to make you feel bad for wanting what you want. There is nothing wrong with wanting something, but manipulating your friends using "I don't know" and the power of veto can break down a relationship.

An alternative to playing the veto power game is to say, "How about if I make the decision?" There is nothing wrong with wanting something. The wanting disorder is a habit from your past that may impact the present, bug your friends and keep you from the togetherness you desire.

A Wise Grandmother

A wise woman took her granddaughter shopping in a toy store and the grandmother said, "I'd like to buy you a toy, so go through the store and pick out something that you would like." The little girl takes off down the aisles and finds something, calling her grandmother over to see it. At the end of the aisle is a magnificent car, a very big, shiny, expensive car. The child says, "I want this." What would most of us do in response to this? "You can't have that!" or "Why do you want that?" or "How about if we look around some more?"

But this grandmother was very wise; she looked at that car and said, "WOW—look at that car. What a beautiful red car, and look at the chrome bumpers, and the leather steering wheel. This is the GREATEST toy in the whole store. I can't afford it, but I'm so proud of you for knowing what you want, and for having such great taste."

In so doing, she validated the little girl for what she wanted, instead of destroying her. She denied the request but honored the child's wanting. The validation process is extremely important. To give a child information is different from telling her that she doesn't want what she, in fact, does want.

It's easy to see how the wanting disorder gets started. It hurts when what you want gets thwarted and perhaps is misunderstood. It's also easy to see how using the manipulation of the veto can help you work around risking an opinion, but it won't help you create togetherness that works. It's important to be able to know what you want and to be able to talk about it. Perhaps it's not easy for you to say "this is what I want" but it is healthy.

We all need a wise grandmother. We all need *to be* a wise grandmother!

The Wanting Disorder
Bulletin Board

It drives me crazy when my girlfriend plays that veto game. I always feel manipulated and it makes me angry. (Mark, 23)

> I totally developed a wanting disorder. I had no idea what I wanted and controlled other people to tell me. I had a mother change my own mind when she did not agree with what I wanted. Fortunately, today I'm aware of when I do it and try to decide for myself. It is still a struggle, though. (Sharon, 29)

I do that! Now I know why. I have a wanting disorder and I
don't want it anymore. (Carole, 19)

> I have spent much energy in my life overriding the negative,
> irresponsible and terrifically damaging messages given to
> me by my depressed parents. I can attest to the existence of
> the wanting disorder. I am now just learning to understand
> what it is I want. With the severe repression of emotions and
> denial of dreams, I am just beginning to ask and see what it
> is I want. (Leona, 44)

Nothing my boyfriend gave me was enough because it wasn't
what I really wanted. (Bonnie, 22)

"What we can't express runs our life." —Anonymous

The Wanting Disorder

Chapter 4

Why, Oh Why, Do I Behave Like That?

"Blame your parents for the way you are; blame yourself if you stay that way."

— Gloria Gallagher

Knowing that our first language is feelings may help us understand why we continue behaving in an automatic way that sometimes sabotages our best opportunities. Is there an error in your thinking?

I know better! Why do I keep doing this to myself? There must be a reason for doing this. How can I stop doing what I don't want to do? My friends don't understand my behavior either. I'm a good person, why do I stay with such losers? Sound familiar? Have you ever wondered about this?

Oh my, the unconscious has such a peculiar strong hold on us. By definition, the unconscious does its own thing without our being able to control it or even know when it is operating. We gave our unconscious its operating instructions long ago and now it operates and runs our life like an autopilot, just under our radar.

Here's how it got its power:

1. **Feelings** were our first language. We had feelings about our earliest experiences that shaped us for better or for worse. Everything sorted itself out with the feelings that we experienced while interacting with people, places and things—all the nouns in our lives.

2. As these feelings emerged, we began to think about what those feelings meant to us. The more we thought about them, the more we tried to make sense of those feelings. Sometimes the **thinking** was accurate. Sometimes the thinking had errors in it.

3. Regardless, a pattern emerged and our thinking led to some **emotional conclusions**.
   - I am a good person. I am talented. I am happy.
   - I am not a good person. I am not wanted. People don't like me.
   - I trust/don't trust others.
   - I am worthwhile/worthless.

It is our feelings that led us to our way of thinking, which in turn led to our patterns and emotional conclusions.

4. A **strategy** emerges from those emotional conclusions—a strategy for dealing with situations. This strategy becomes an operating system that works in conjunction with the unconscious. In a given situation, the operating system automatically turns on, and the behaviors learned in those original circumstances are activated.

If the original thinking was accurate, the **operating system** and emotional conclusions will be on the healthy side. If there was an error in thinking, the operating system and emotional conclusions will lead to dysfunctional behaviors.

Sound simple? Let's apply it to the opening paragraph of this chapter. I know better, why do I keep doing this to myself?
   - I'm a worthy person, why do I keep ending up with such losers?
   - If I can't afford to shop, why do I keep shopping and spending?
   - If I am attracted to the wrong kind of people, why do I keep going back for more grief?

- I know this has something to do with my childhood, why can't I get beyond it?

Let's take, for example, someone whose father or mother was an alcoholic and whose behavior was erratic, or abusive, or angry. As a five-year-old child, the reaction to such behavior was to believe that the behavior of the other person was related in some way to what that five-year-old did or who she was. Therefore, if she (as the child) behaved in a certain way, Mom/Dad would stop drinking, or love more or stop being abusive.

Decades later, as an adult, the feelings are still there. The thinking is that of the five-year-old. The emotional conclusions were the best the five-year-old child could come up with. The strategies that emerged were also from the five-year-old child's mind and usually were designed to avoid pain and confusion.

The strategies became locked into the unconscious and are no longer consciously activated. Years later, the adult reacts to an alcoholic man/woman or any painful or confusing situation in much the same way they did as a five-year-old. Rather than confront inappropriate behavior in their mate or date or friend, they avoid the confrontation, and somehow think that the problem is theirs to solve rather than the alcoholic's poor choices. In short, they become confused as to who owns the problem. They stay in an unhealthy relationship instead of walking away from it because the internal five-year-old is calling the shots.

So, when you've asked yourself, "Why do I behave like that?" the explanation goes back to our earliest experiences.

As babies, we experience feelings. I'm uncomfortable. I'm hungry. I'm wet. I'm demanding and when I am rescued with being fed, changed and responded to, I feel held and safe. Babies cry and let Mom translate those cries into meeting the baby's needs.

To understand our behavior is to know and understand

that our first language is feelings. From infancy, we feel things that happen to us and around us and our bodies and minds take in nonverbal information. As we grow, we begin to question what it all means. We are becoming who we are—emerging as individuals.

As we begin to think about our experiences, we make stuff up about our feelings and add labels and language to those feelings. Thinking becomes our second language. Yet, feelings are accurate. What we do with the thoughts about our feelings as we grow determines, in many ways, the quality of our adult lives.

Do we trust our feelings as adults? Can we learn to trust them? Many adults reject, ignore, edit or translate those feelings so that they will go away or suit the situation they are in without having to SEE what is happening to them. Our experiences with our feelings reflect other people's responses to us. And the big question continues, begun in infancy, "Am I safe here?"

From our thinking about experiences, we draw some emotional conclusions and, as we develop, the emotional conclusions lead us to organize our lives around those conclusions. Some of these conclusions reached in childhood are now unconscious yet become the major organizers or operating systems of our lives. Consider the following all too common adolescent example.

An adolescent girl is attracted to a young man and they have sexual feelings toward each other. While not recommended in adolescence, they have sexual intercourse and the feelings that go along with that experience (good, bad, confusing, etc). She begins to think about those feelings and thinks, "We just had sex, and people who have sex are making love so therefore this must be love." She comes to the emotional conclusion that she must be in love.

Being in love becomes the organizing principle for her life

and she plans for happily ever after assuming that since she feels this way, it must be love. Because of this belief, she makes many of her decisions around this relationship. She may choose her classes to be with him. Her choice of a college or career could be directly related to his plans rather than creating some of her own. In short, her thinking (and the too early sexual experience) has organized her behavior.

The young man may or may not feel the same way about her. That is, he may reach a different emotional conclusion about their sexual interaction. If, for him, it was just sex, her involvement and commitment to this relationship may be confusing to him.

If there was an error in her thinking about her feelings and the sexual experience she had, there is also an error in her emotional conclusion and in her organizing principle for her life. In short, maybe it was just sex. But she is stuck with the feelings, the thinking, and the experience as she has translated it and the future that seems to go along with too early sexual experimentation.

This is not an uncommon development. Many young women have given their futures away with just such errors in thinking (and too early sexual experiences).

Making Assumptions Leads to Misunderstandings

Have you ever jumped to a conclusion? Have you ever been wrong with that conclusion?

Maybe the following scenario has happened to you.

You schedule a lunch date and the other person doesn't show up. She is late and you begin to think "Why isn't she here? How dare she be late? She was supposed to be here at noon and it's a quarter after, and this is rude, but she's still coming." That's the belief system.

By 12:30 you're thinking she might be hurt or you have the wrong day and it's your error. "Why isn't she here? Maybe she didn't want to come. What kind of friend is she if she didn't want to come? She's not dependable, she's not trustworthy and I'm not important to her." All of these thoughts go through your mind. Those are your emotional conclusions. Because of that you begin to say things like, "I'm never meeting anyone for lunch again. Everyone in the world lets me down. I can't trust anyone. I'm not going to call her until she calls me—that's that!"

All of these thoughts started with your feelings of being ignored, left alone or left out. Next, you thought about the situation in a variety of ways; and then you organized what you were going to do next, to retaliate against the person and all other people like them!

This works beautifully unless there is an error in your thinking. There is never an error in your feelings, and your body senses more than your brain does. It senses tension, fear, dishonesty, all kinds of things. The challenge is to think clearly about the feelings.

Sometimes, even though you know better, you try to override your feelings. You think things like, "I didn't feel that," "I didn't see that." The truth is you don't want to see that, so you don't—which becomes your conclusion. If you don't trust your feelings, you're probably going to have an error in your thinking.

The error in your thinking may lead you to say, "Well, that's just the way I am! I'm never having lunch with anyone again." Then, along the way, someone else invites you to lunch and you decline, saying, "I don't do lunch."

Let's revisit how the unconscious gets us from waiting for fifteen minutes to "I don't do lunch." Our operating systems/ organizing principles are active in our unconscious. That is, given certain situations, we match up new experiences with old responses that have become automatic and we no longer see things clearly.

Probably the best explanation of the unconscious comes from Mary Lynne Musgrove, an exceptional career counselor:

The unconscious is unconscious—therefore, by definition, it is not available for us to know. It is like a storage tank with a lid on it. You can't know what is in yours . . . It is all the painful feelings you didn't dare to feel. It is full of feelings that are not safe for us to feel. In this storage tank you've stored up all the feelings that you don't want to feel.

The unconscious is all about self-defense. When those painful feelings are stirred up, the unconscious is triggered, the door flies open and the person falls in. We go in there in order to protect ourselves. "I don't want to feel this; I don't want to know it." We don't know why, but that's how the unconscious works. It is designed to protect us.

So the unconscious is like an automatic pilot that causes us to jump to conclusions or automatically behave a certain way when a situation matches up with our previous experiences. It is something like a somatic reflex arc. Do you remember that from your biology class?

Our bodies have a nervous system, which has two routes. One route allows for an experience to send a message to the brain so that the brain can make a decision and respond. The other, and the one that I think applies here, is the reflex arc where, for example, we touch something hot and immediately pull our hand away. It happens automatically because the sensation goes to the spinal cord and sends a message immediately back to the hand. This bypasses the brain input completely.

Our "organizing principle" or operating system works in much the same way. It is a reflex arc, bypassing the brain, and going to automatic behavior, learned from some other experience, perhaps long ago. The patterns we fall into may always be to respond defensively whether it's appropriate or not. Perhaps we are always angry or always afraid, whether or not it's appropriate. Perhaps any criticism leads us to depression. Perhaps the pattern is always to respond with optimism or pessimism but the "always" response is what will limit a healthy response to a given situation. In a sense, we become automatic responders instead of responding independently in a situation.

Our thoughts organize experiences throughout development in a positive way, provided they meet with affirming, accepting and containing responses from caregivers. The key is steady, tuned-in responsiveness.

If we are in a situation at home or at work that is not affirming, accepting and supportive, there may be an injury to the spirit and selfhood of the individual. We ponder, are the people at work the problem or is it me?

The areas of feelings, thought, self and spirit can relate directly to self-esteem issues. If the self is wounded, then the spirit doesn't thrive. Perhaps then, we can say that to reach the higher states of consciousness, we absolutely need to have clear thinking about the emotions we experience. This is not such an easy task.

With the above mentioned examples in mind, I repeat the question, "Why do I behave like that?" The answer is not a simple one. Answers are found in asking the right questions. Here are some you can ask yourself.

▶ In reviewing experiences or patterns with friends, co-workers, partners and loved ones, what are the things you do that do not make sense?

▶ Can you think of a time when you reached a conclusion that now seems questionable to you?

▶ Can you revisit some of your earlier experiences and relationships and see them from a different perspective? Do you see a pattern?

▶ Can you look at some of the patterns in your life that you do not enjoy repeating? What do they have in common?

▶ What will it take to make the changes you want?

This is a good place to journal your thoughts.

ACTION ITEM ·········▶

Puzzling

On this page is a jumble of numbers. Your task is to connect them in order. Connect them in order, 1, 2, 3, etc. See how many numbers you can connect in one-and-a-half minutes. When you have finished, circle the highest number you reached... 18, 24, 26. Then turn the page for the discussion of the activity and your next instructions.

```
1         37              26  40
      53                  38
27        5               6       18
          51
          15      50
49                                30
      29
                  52      2
25  39  41                14  28
                                  42
3   13                    54
                 4        16
17


      31        60  10
57    35  45     20  46
      19                      24
23        43                  32
      9
      7   47     22  36
55
          11                  12
      59                      56
                 58      34
33        21                  48
                 44
```

You may have found this to be a frustrating activity because it's not in order—it's jumbled—you had to overlap. You may be frustrated because you didn't have enough time to finish. It wasn't easy because the numbers are not in order. Some people even beat themselves up because they feel stupid and have trouble doing it. What were you thinking? Did you wonder why you were doing this? Is it a trick? Did you feel competitive pressure doing it? If so, WHY?

Did you begin to notice anything while you were performing this activity? There was a pattern. Odd numbers were on the left, and the even numbers were on the right. Another pattern was by sixes—groups of six—six on the top and then six on the bottom.

Now that you've noticed the patterns, connect the numbers again. You have one-and-a-half minutes to repeat the exercise. Stop after ninety seconds and circle the highest number you reach.

```
1            37              26   40
       53                    38
27            5                   18
             51
             15      50
49                                30
       29                    2
                     52
25   39   41                 14   28
                                  42
3    13                      54
                     4       16
17


       31            60   10
57     35    45       20   46
       19                         24
23           43                   32
       9                 8
       7     47      22   36
55                                12
             11                   56
       59                34
                     58           48
33           21
                     44
```

(Source Unknown)

Did you improve this time? What was different for you? You knew where to look and that there was a pattern. You had a visual memory of where you'd been. You knew it wasn't a trick. There was an order to it. What seemed random began to have an order. So what we begin to notice is that we can navigate something even if originally it looks like a hodge-podge.

If there is a system and a pattern, and we can navigate it more successfully, the frustration level goes down. It's not random anymore. We know where to go next.

Navigating numbers is simple compared to navigating relationships. Understanding what works and what hurts and how to fix what is broken gives us a way to navigate relationships more successfully. What works and what hurts can bring up feelings and thoughts about our relationships in the past as well as guide us to what we want to create in the future that is different.

Why, Oh Why, Do I Behave Like That?

Bulletin Board

I learned that I have an effect on everyone. My insults hurt them, my hand heals them, my Kleenex dries their tears, my arms rock and my fists bruise. I make an impact on everyone I meet and I want it to be a positive impact. (Martha, 37)

> Knowing how you feel is good but to actually understand why and where these feelings came from, or more so, whom you learned them from is a powerful life tool. Knowing this, it kind of feels like I have an edge on people. I'm able to relate better to others and understand them more at any point in their lives. Whether someone needs to be held, understood, or even to be validated, I can help out in some way. (Alan, 23)

It amazes me how resilient the human mind and heart can be when seeking to survive in a hostile environment. Even though I grew up largely unheld, unattached, molested and beaten down, I now have the opportunity to learn, grow and move beyond the terror and limitations of my childhood. I can choose to understand my emotional and psychological challenges, and fill my life and the lives of others with hope, responsiveness, passion and praise. (Fiona, 30)

> My father was and still is a very unaffectionate man, highly critical, emotionally reserved and a workaholic. I cannot remember a time when he hugged me or asked me how my day went. Work was everything to him, and the rest of the family felt that strongly. The one time I hugged him as I left for college, he stood stiffly with his arms to his side. I believe he feels deeply, but is unable to express emotions. His father passed away when he was five, and he grew up in poverty. He has not been able to deal with his past and lives "emotionally impoverished" as an adult, rarely showing joy or celebration. (Kalei, 26)

I was fed and clothed, but I did not receive the attention or warmth a child needs to grow. As a small child, I was left for hours, unattended, with restraints, while my parents worked on the farm. I was not a wanted child. I used to feel empty. (Darren, 37)

> I like having a sense of community around me, my friendships have always been very important to me. My negative feelings about my family feel more like something I want to run away from. It is interesting that I am thirty-eight years old and I have not created a family of my own. Part of that has been a conscious decision not to do it the same way my parents did and I think I have gone to the opposite extreme and denied myself the experience. (Katy, 38)

I have learned that I get the life that goes with my attitude. I have control of my attitude, and can alter my life in a more positive way, which then reflects a better image to my family and friends. I feel better about myself, about who I am and where I am going and I strive to create the attitude that brings about a fuller and more joyful life for myself and others with whom I have relationships. (Bart, 29)

> If I don't show my son enough love and support, what kind of person will he grow up to be? Would he make a good friend, a good husband, a good father? (Doreen, 24)

I believe my parents did the best they could with the skills they had. (Ulee, 36)

> I remember these struggles as a little boy—like they happened yesterday. I need so much work and healing. (Steve, 29)

I vacillate, or regress, from being a chronological adult to an emotional child. As an adult, I find myself asking, what do I need and want in a relationship? Only to find myself reacting as a child, very fearfully. (Mattie, 37)

> The hard work of giving ourselves this care we never got as children is the difference between living and just surviving. (Terry, 42)

"By seeking and blundering we learn."

—Goethe

I live in my shell
    Inside a box
Under the floor
Of a house of stone
Hidden deep in a forest. . .
I'm safe from you here.

You could find me
    If you really loved me.

Chapter 5

Grounding and Holding

"Your mother carried you inside her for nine months: You carry her inside you...forever."

— Oprah Winfrey

We all need to be held from infancy into adulthood by someone or some thing. As infants, we need to be held to keep from falling. As adults, the need changes so that we feel the need to be held in order to keep us from falling apart.

When a mother carries her infant and enters a crowded room, all eyes turn and begin to smile at the darling "beginner person." There is a softening and a quiet that fills the room.

What is it that captures and enraptures everyone's attention in an almost sacred Aaahhhh? Don't you sometimes wish that as an adult, there were the chance of that kind of acceptance for you?

ACTION ITEM ··········▶

Connecting with an Infant

If you've not been near an infant in some time, try to hook up with one through a friend or relative, and keep in mind this chapter's content as you observe your relationship with the baby. Don't try to remember or imagine what it feels like; you must do this in person. Your memory just won't do it!

If you already have an infant, continue to enjoy and observe the miracle with regard to your bond with this precious child.

As you hold the baby, ask yourself:

▶ Does he like to be held? (How do you know that?)

▶ Does the baby know you and recognize you? (How do you know?)

▶ How do you feel when you are holding her?

▶ How do you know when he has been held long enough?

▶ Does she react differently to different people holding her?

What you as the holder provide is safety and protection. In return, what you may experience is the tingling feeling of warmth and response to the baby's skin and the eye contact that come with holding. Many of those who hold report feeling significant in the role of protector.

The infant is fully dependent on the holder's commitment and caring, competence in supporting his head and holding him safe, and protecting him during this most vulnerable time.

Observe the differences in holding styles and see the strength in most relationships between mother and child.

Here's the rub: Children do not get to choose their holders or parents or significant ones in the beginning. Sometimes, children are not held "good enough" either physically or emotionally, and sense that something is missing even into adulthood. Other times, children are blessed with good holding parents and benefit from that for the rest of their lives.

If you hold an infant out away from your body with the baby's legs dangling, at first they will look around curiously, but then their little feet will begin searching for something to support them. This demonstrates the built-in need to feel grounded and the need to feel secure and supported.

So what is it about holding that seems to be the grounding for people-growing? Since we do not have a choice in the quality or quantity of holding we receive as an infant, what can we do as adults if we believe that we did not get good enough holding?

What Is Good Enough?

When I ask parents if they are good enough parents, they are sometimes offended and say that they would not settle for just good enough. To the question "Did you give or get good enough holding?" they might respond "definitely not." You see, the problem with good enough is that it is erroneously compared with perfect. And none of us are that!

Actually, good enough is a great goal. Let me share this explanation. Picture a houseplant in your home. If you over water or under water that plant, it will die. If you water it good enough it will live. It doesn't need perfect watering to survive. Some plants require very little water to look great. Others require lots of water. So perfect watering or perfect holding or perfect parenting is a standard that in reality is inappropriate or doesn't actually exist.

What does exist is the need for good enough parenting and good enough holding based on the child's needs. If they get good enough holding, they will grow. If your parenting is good enough, they will grow. It is important as parents to tune in to the needs of your children, and to hold and parent as best you can. Yes, you can learn more about this. You can grow into the parent you want your children to have.

It is also important to remember that the perfection standard will just get in the way of enjoying your children. Beating yourself up about an inappropriate standard will take energy away from focusing on what your child actually needs.

This experience of holding and being held is the most primary and the most difficult to put into words. It is where we get our start. The holding experience is difficult to describe, but extremely important for our being.

Who or What Holds You?

The experience of feeling arms around us, and a sense that these are strong arms — that somehow they are strong enough to keep us from falling — is the sense of being held.

Perhaps the most powerful example of the healing touch of a hug is in the story of the preemie twins that has flashed around the Internet. Did you hear the story? If you do a Google search for "rescuing hug," you will see a photo taken by Chris Christo of the *Worcester Telegram and Gazette* that speaks volumes about the power of holding.

Twins were born who weighed about two pounds each at birth. Both of them were in their own incubator at the beginning of life. One of the twins was stronger and healthier than the other and the weaker of the two cried a lot, gasped for air and was not expected to live. On a particularly bad day, nothing seemed to calm her, so the newborn intensive care unit nurse, who had exhausted all measures to help her, finally put the stronger twin in the same incubator with her little sister.

The stronger twin snuggled up to the weaker one, threw her arm around her and, remarkably, the weaker twin's blood-oxygen saturation levels, which had been frighteningly low, soared. She began to breathe more easily. The frantic crying stopped and her normal pinkish color quickly returned.

Over the next weeks, the weaker twin's health improved steadily in her new, shared quarters. The children survived their rocky beginning and in time went home with their parents.

I spoke with Chris Christo, the photographer. He was invited by the family into the intensive care unit and, in the blink of an eye, captured that remarkable moment and gifted the world with a photo that hangs in homes and offices around the globe and shows up in over ten thousand websites. Check it out!

We continue to learn more and more about the tremendous

physiological benefits of being held. But there is more to holding that we need to understand. The sense of holding exists between our fantasies and our experienced reality. When we're little, we believe that our parents can protect us from everything; they are big and strong, so they will certainly protect us. As we grow up, we realize that they are ungrounded too.

An example of how grounding works in the physical world might make sense. When we plug electrical things into the wall, there are three prongs; one of them is a "ground." We have a "ground" to keep us from being shocked. It protects us. The holding experience is a grounding experience. Holding protects us.

We look around when we're outside and we have the sense that the earth is holding us up. We feel comfortable with the earth as support and take it for granted that it will stay where it is, until we have an earthquake—at which time we have a little less confidence. (We have earthquakes in California.)

A young woman told me that during an earthquake she had her boyfriend's arms around her and she was feeling secure. It was wonderful. She thanked him and asked him how he felt. He responded he was holding on for dear life; he was scared to death!

It's a fantasy that the other person is holding us; the reality is that they too are ungrounded. That is, they are doing the best they can, and are also in need of being held.

The holding experience comes in two parts: the holder, and the holdee. Both are experiencing holding in a completely different way. The quality of the holding experience resides in the one being held. No matter the intent of the hug, the recipient determines whether the hug or holding is meeting their needs.

Let's Look at Hugs

Have you ever had a wonderful hug? Have you ever had a

sleazy hug? What is a sleazy hug? Is it manipulative? Is it controlling? Is it unwelcome? What is it that makes you snuggle into some hugs and other times feel like you are involved in a sleazy deal? Somehow, you sense and know the difference and it's an internal response.

Who determines whether or not it's a good hug? You do. No one else has a say.

No matter what it looks like on the outside to an observer, the meaning of the hug is always determined internally. The key is in the receiver of the hug. It has to do with safety. It depends on your feelings, therefore YOU decide. This is an inside or internal experience.

The other person can be offering what they consider to be a genuine hug, but if you do not receive it that way or do not want it, then in your mind it isn't pleasant. It can still feel uncomfortable to you regardless of the hugger's intentions. There are going to be times when you know you don't like a hug, but you don't know why. My advice to you is to trust your instincts. If there is something you don't like, there is a reason you're getting that message. It's okay to say, "I don't want you to do this." When it's a family member, it's more difficult to find a polite way to say, "Get away from me."

Men are sometimes afraid to hug other men because they think their actions will be misinterpreted as a sexual overture. Really, they miss out on a normal connection that they could enjoy. Different cultures have different rules about touching and physical closeness. In some cultures, men and women greet each other with a hug and a kiss on both cheeks. There are some families who don't touch or hug much. For whatever reason, they limit physical contact.

I knew a young man from an Arab country who told me that no one in his home country touches. He was struck by what seemed to be a huggy-touchy college campus where many students regularly greeted each other with hugs. When asked how he liked it here with all this hugging, he replied, "I LIKE IT HERE!"

We like to be held, to be touched. Being held, if it's a good hug, gives us a sense of strong arms around us that keep us from falling. Our sense of holding exists between fantasy and reality because a lot of it happens inside us — in our heads and in our guts. We react viscerally. We have a sensation and we determine if this is good, welcome, a comfort — or not.

Almost unconsciously, adults make a decision based on the perceived emotional strength of the holder. I will not let you hold me if I do not sense that you're strong enough to do that. And you won't let me hold you if you sense that I'm not strong enough. The strength is an emotional strength, not a physical strength.

You may be willing to hold others, but not willing to let them hold you because you don't trust that they are strong enough, in whatever way, to really keep you safe — to hold you. It's a very important distinction that we make. And we sense it, just as the baby senses it.

At the heart of the holding experience is a set of expectations based on what happened to us when we were young. This may be conscious or unconscious depending on how aware we were. We all need to be held. When the holding is good, we want more and more.

The first three years of life are so significant. The sense of security that comes from good enough holding during that time is key. It's tough not to get the holding right away. The infant is not able to say, "Gee, I don't think I'm getting good enough holding here." It affects their ability to venture out and to have confidence in themselves and in the world.

I will not let you hold me if I don't think you're strong enough to do it. The lack of early good enough holding can create a pattern of expecting not to be held. If one gets used to the fact that people aren't very strong, they start sending out the message that they don't think they want to be held. "I don't think you can; I don't think anyone can, so I'd better be self-contained."

If you get to the point where you cannot trust the holding other, then your sense is that they will drop you. Another way of saying that is, "I don't think they are trustworthy." Or we could create a new word: they are not hold-worthy. When you are fearful that they can't hold you, you decide not to take any chances.

If you realize or believe that you have not been held good enough, there is still hope. If you want to be held, pick someone who you believe is strong enough to hold you and stay away from emotionally weak or abusive people.

In contrast to your experience as a child, as an adult you have the choice to select the people you want in your life and who you want to hold you. It's important to carefully select the people who hold you, because when you ground your existence in them, they have the ability or potential to either hold (or contain) you, or to traumatize you. You want to be careful about whom you pick.

Keep in mind that people are imperfect. At the same time you begin to ground your existence in others, you have to consider that they too have their limits. Remember, holding exists between fantasy and reality. You may believe that a person will hold you all the time, and always be there for you, but then what if they let you down? They may not have done it on purpose, but they still let you down. Then you have to decide if they're allowed that mistake, or if you will never let them hold you again. You adjust.

Holding Systems

Holding can be more than a physical act. As we grow, the protective holding changes to other forms. We can be held by family, by friends, by belief systems, by ideals, by classrooms and teachers and sometimes by addictions. Habits and schedules can hold us. If I sense that I am held, then my belief is that the world will hold me.

When people don't feel held, they often turn to drugs or alcohol or cigarettes as the holding system. Jim Beam or Jack Daniels becomes their best friend!

The Classroom

A classroom holds us while we learn. Have you ever been in a class where everyone was really involved with high engagement and energy and excitement? That is an example of *being held* in a classroom.

What is it in a classroom that makes it safe to answer out loud what we are thinking or to risk being wrong? Perhaps the answer comes when we remember all the classrooms where we did NOT feel safe enough to speak out or to venture opinions. What was different in the safe ones? Perhaps the key difference is whether it is a safe place to be wrong.

I have asked students if they remembered a situation in a classroom where they did not feel safe and almost every hand went up. They shared sad stories about feeling put down, of being embarrassed or of feeling humiliated when they tried unsuccessfully to participate. Has that ever happened to you? This is a tragedy in education because in any classroom, we hold each other while we learn.

One student, Talia, said, "I had a hard time keeping up with my classmates. A tremendous feeling of anxiety came over me every time the teacher called on me. The teacher would snap at every mistake I made and got so impatient with me that she would try and rush me through the work. From then on, school has been a very frightening place for me. I still struggle to overcome these feelings of being intimidated and insecure with myself."

In every classroom, the wrong answer is the right answer to a different question!

Meaning Systems

We also have meaning systems that hold us. An ideal can be a system. What are some examples of a meaning system? A church, a team, work, a sorority, a club, a philosophy, exercise habits, a marriage, our belief systems, the system of truth.

We are held by these different concepts. There are some people who may not have been held physically but the church holds them, or they are held by a spiritual belief system. The system then, a meaning system, begins to hold us.

You would be wise to invest in some of the holding systems available to you: religion, AA, spiritual beliefs, a job, a relationship, a commitment to a charity — something that you believe in. For example, belief that hard work and a commitment to excellence will be rewarded holds us as we participate in a world that doesn't always make sense. Respecting our elders is a tradition in almost every culture in the world. We believe in "believing in them" and that holds us as we find our way in our family and community.

When the Holding Fails

Sometimes a person who has held us betrays us or lets us down big time. We lose not only the person who held us, but also everything that being held by them gave us. This might include self-confidence, self-esteem, etc. We begin to question everything they said to us and about us. For example, "If he's a liar, does this mean that I am NOT all the nice things he said about me, like I'm beautiful, talented and wonderful?" And conversely, "If she is a liar, then perhaps that means I'm NOT as bad as she said I was!"

Sometimes the same thing happens with a belief system because, like humans, belief systems can be fragile. Perhaps we have grown up with a spiritual belief and something happens to cause us to question it.

For example, a spiritual leader fails us. Suddenly we are

questioning the system. If the person represents a belief system, does that mean we experience a loss of faith? Many religious groups are facing legitimate challenges. For a while it is like an earthquake, the ground has given way beneath us. We can lose confidence in the world and our family and our faith. They have held us and now we're questioning it. In our own new way, we're trying to sort it out.

Issues from Lack of Holding

When the ground moves, whether it's an earthquake or at a time when our belief system changes, we feel unstable, unheld. When we feel held, we can venture into the future with confidence. The opposite is also true. If we do not feel held, we have trouble realistically planning for the future—we stay right where we are and feel immobilized.

A former high school friend had a son with special needs. As we talked about her life as a single parent, I asked how she had set things up to take care of him in the future. She answered that he'd have to take care of himself. I asked if she had insurance or something set up to take care of him if anything happened to her. No. Nothing. She was living day to day with no sense of the future, only of the present. What I learned as we talked was that in her family, she never felt held. She never felt quite good enough despite the fact that she was an excellent student and popular in high school.

When we feel held, we can look into the future. When we are not held, we do not look into the future. Instead, we have the sense of it only being right now, in the present, and that's it. My friend was a strong example of a person with no sense of future.

When we have someone who believes in us and who is behind us, we feel supported; we feel held. This can be a friend, a teacher or coach, our family, or someone who at the right place and the right time passes a word of encouragement on to us.

Leo Buscaglia, professor and author known affectionately as "Dr. Hug," spoke to the holding experience when he said, "Too often we underestimate the power of a touch, a smile, a kind word, a listening ear, an honest compliment, or the smallest act of caring, all of which have the potential to turn a life around."

Refueling and Holding

Refueling is touching base. It is best seen in a small child who ventures away from his mother, then suddenly realizes that he has wandered away from her and runs back, grabbing her leg with all his might.

We touch base in many ways. Think about some of the things you do. You might call up your friends and say things like, "I just wanted to touch base and hear your voice. Yeah, everything is fine — nothing I really wanted to talk about."

What you're doing is refueling, touching base and reaching out to get grounded again. "It's been a really rough day and I just wanted to hear your voice." It's the same as grabbing on to your mother's leg for just a moment and then venturing out again. You do this to feel held.

Ellen and the Big But

Look at the example of Ellen. She spent many years trying to understand the contradictions in the way she was parented.

She was held, hugged and kissed. Her mother always told her how wonderful she was and how much she loved her. She would say, "Every Mommy should have an Ellen."

"BUT," Ellen says, "She couldn't protect me. She couldn't protect me from being abused. She really loved me, yet I was beaten every day of my young life by my older sister. My mother's energy went into trying to hold together a family with an out of control older sibling. I was an unfortunate casualty of a war I didn't understand."

The story of Ellen is a story of contradictions and the "BIG

BUT." Here is someone who was told time and again how special she was and how loved she was BUT she was not protected. She was not safe. Because she couldn't protect her, Ellen's mother left her vulnerable. And Ellen's emotional conclusion from looking at what was happening was this: "If parents don't protect you, then you're not really important to them. I felt love, affection and approval, but not holding."

Anytime you hear the word BUT, notice it and know that you've just cancelled out anything you heard before that. "I love you, BUT." Pay attention. All that precedes the word "but" evaporates; pay careful attention to everything that is said after the BUT.

- "You are a very special person, BUT."
- "She told me how wonderful I was, BUT."
- "I got a lot of love from my mother, BUT she was either unwilling or unable to protect me."

Swamped with the care and support of four children, Ellen's mother was overwhelmed as a single mother.

As we grow we develop certain expectations of how the world operates in relation to us. "If I am held, I internalize the idea that the world will be responsive to me. If I'm not adequately held, then I might believe the opposite."

Sex and Holding

It's easier to ask for sex than it is to ask for holding. Think about it. For some reason, "Do you want to have sex?" is a much more comfortable request than "Would you hold me?" There are a lot of people having sex when what they really want is to be held.

If what you really want is to be held and you're having sex instead, how do you feel? Perhaps the answer is:

- Unsatisfied? (Because what you're getting is not what you wanted),
- Empty? (because you've asked for what you really didn't

want in order to get what you thought you were going to get, and it's not the same),

- Cheap? (because you have given away your precious self. Feeling cheap, is emotionally expensive).

Perhaps you think it's not COOL to ask to be held; it's COOL to ask for sex. If we ask to be held, we are afraid people will think we're needy. We *are* needy. Having needs is a part of being human. Being held can give confidence and security. Sex doesn't necessarily give security. If that's not what I really wanted, when I'm through, I won't be satisfied.

As a counselor, I've talked with a lot of males who say, "When the sex is over—what then?" They usually wind up saying something like, "Would you go home now," because they didn't get what they wanted either. This is not just a female thing; we're talking about relationships. Sex is not necessarily relational. A sexual *relationship* is complicated and is a great deal more than having sex.

Sex along with holding, and in an appropriate trustworthy relationship, is a whole different form of holding. It is satisfying. It is grounding. It does give us a sense of having a future.

Mothering and Fathering

Mothers are not the only holders. Fathers are holders too. Women are not the only good mothers; sometimes fathers do the mothering much better. There is a language issue here. If I say, "She mothered four children" what does it mean? You might answer "She gave birth; she cared for, loved them, held them and raised four children."

If I say to you, "He fathered four children," what does that mean to you? A common response is, "Sperm donor." This then is followed by laughter. We say he fathered and then we laugh because we don't assign the same nurturing to the father as we do to the mother. Is that fair?

An individual male is capable of doing wonderful holding

and nurturing of a child. The mother may not be the primary holder and nurturer. But we tend as a culture to treat it that way; it's a bad rap for men, and something as a culture we need to work on. There are a great many single women and men raising children and parenting. In our culture, both men and women need to be respected for their ability to hold and to nurture.

Failure to Thrive

Failure to thrive describes a baby who is failing to gain weight and grow as expected. Diagnosing and treating a child who fails to thrive focuses on identifying any underlying problem and promoting weight gain. From there, doctors and the family work together to get the child back into a healthy growth pattern. Generally, the child requires a great deal of holding. If babies are not held or touched enough, they will die.

You may have seen programs on TV that discuss orphanages with too many infants to tend. They leave the children alone to sleep and they are not touched or held. Many of them die if they just lie there. So what does the baby need? Touching, holding and a loving parent.

When the diagnosis is failure to thrive, people need to hold that baby around the clock, feed him and touch him while he's sleeping. It may be that is what it takes for the infant to exist as a person—to have a sense of self and to live.

Lack of Holding

Think about the following example in light of what you now know about the importance of holding. Think of how you would feel if these were the messages you received from your mother or father.

- "Your dad wanted me to have an abortion."
- "I could have been very successful in life but you came along."
- "You really don't count for anything here."

Or maybe you can relate to one of the following experiences:

- "We moved thirty times before I was fourteen. Each move meant a different school."
- "I never had any friends."
- "Dad dropped me off for a visitation with Mom and never came back."
- "My folks were always stoned and they hit us a lot."
- "I had four stepfathers."
- "If we asked for attention from Mom, our stepfather called us little whores and little bastards."
- "I started doing bad things. I used Speed, lost twenty pounds, got paranoid, stayed inside the house and couldn't think anymore."
- "I was barely maintaining."

How could a person with any of these experiences possibly have felt held?

Holding Language

Holding is a frequently used concept in our language. How many ways can you think of where we use the word hold in our everyday language? Some examples follow:

- Hold on — don't give up
- On hold — telephone language
- Held back — restricted by others — not promoted in school or a job
- Hold over — threaten
- Held over — continued on until another time
- Hold in — keeping feelings inside
- Hold on there — wait
- Hold up — restore another, or robbery
- Holding tank — where drunks or other suspects are kept
- Hold or fold — cards
- Hold — stocks

- To have and to hold—wedding vows

Holding Questions to Think About

▶ What is it about holding others and being held ourselves that is so indefinably special?

▶ When we say "Do you want or need a hug?" are we really saying, "I want to give you a hug." What is it that makes us shy enough to always put the need on them? As the holder, we say that we are helping the other person who needs it and, yet, we ourselves are receiving the benefits of human contact as we extend our help to the other.

▶ Is there joy in reviewing baby pictures that show us being held, and special and loved?

▶ What is it about being held that quiets everything down and allows us to venture out again into the real world?

▶ What if we determine that we do not feel held by anyone or anything or that we never felt held? What can we do about it?

▶ What does it take to be held well or to hold another person well?

Being held good enough may have been your first experience of togetherness that works. Alternately, not being held good enough may have been your earliest or deepest hurt. Now that you understand how holding can impact your life, you can better choose people and systems to hold you and, in return, offer "good enough" holding to others.

ACTION ITEM ··········▶

Mapping Your Relationships

Return to your relationship maps and mark an H for holding on the circles that represent those who really held you.

Are there some people you have held? Identify them with a different style of H.

I grew up in a violent and unstable household where there was some sporadic physical holding, but no emotional protection or support provided by either of my parents. (Fiona, 30)

> Before I met my wife, I never felt held and wasn't interested in the future. (Raj, 29)

I am blessed to have my grandmother. Her skin is as white as any Caucasian, her hair straight, her eyes graying-blue, but her soul is that of an African woman. One would never know from her outward appearance that she is Black, but the history locked in her mind and in her heart clearly defines who she is. Her grandmother was a slave and the history passed down from generation to generation holds me. The courage of my ancestors gives me strength. It gives me a sense of having strong loving arms around me. I have endured cruelty in my lifetime, cruelty too painful for me to even write about, but I survived because of the sense of there-ness that I felt from my family. I knew I could count on their love to prevail. It gave me the containment and the support that I needed. (Ella, 27)

> I love the innocence of children . . . I wish someone had protected me. (Susan, 24)

I like the feeling of knowing that someone cares about how I feel, what I need and what I want. I like being held and validated. I get a warm feeling just knowing I have plenty of people in my life that I can turn to. (Mary, 26)

> To me nothing calms the body more warmly than to be physically held. As a child I don't remember getting a lot of hugs. In fact, I remember my mother hugging me more as a teenager than as a child. It wasn't that much, yet I can honestly say I never doubted my parents love for me. I felt loved and cared for. (Mercy, 28)

At the ripe old age of twenty I was in a severe car crash and suffered a concussion the size of the Titanic. Waking up I called for my mother. I yearned for her holding and her comfort. The fact that my mother was there for me all through those years, to comfort and ease the pain, actually gave me a lot of self-confidence, and I feel like I can do anything. (Shawn, 22)

> I'd never felt that I was being held by my father until I came alone to the U.S. eight months ago. I could feel his affection for me, but I didn't really like him. I thought I could live without him forever. But when I talked with him on the phone after coming to this country, I realized that I'm being held by him, not only financially, but also emotionally. (Jin, 20)

Holding? I don't remember any. In the meager defense of my parents, common child rearing techniques at the time were odd. Don't pick up babies too much! You'll spoil them. Bottle-feeding was encouraged over breast-feeding.... How convenient! Times have certainly changed. However, neither of my parents was inclined to be particularly parental. I don't ever recall either parent holding or consoling my brother or myself, and I certainly never witnessed the slightest sign of affection between the two of them. Conversely, we were always a pet-owning household and the pets enjoyed full family member status and were lavished with affection and attention by all. (Felix, 41)

> I remember holding my son when he was a tiny baby, and how powerful it was to have a baby "sink in" to me. I wonder if my mom had that experience of me—or my father. I know how important it was to me as a parent. I still try to hug my son as much as possible, and I am so grateful he is available to it. (Donald, 40)

Holding—this chapter was a tough one for me because I had to face the realization that I'd never been held as a child. The reflection on my childhood allowed me to open up doors (padlocked fortress doors) that had been shut for quite a while. (Inga, 26)

My mother made it a point to tell me when I was less than ten years old that my father had wanted her to abort her pregnancy at eighteen years old—that would have been me. I guess she wanted me to know that she saved me, but I have never lost the sense that I was not wanted. (Twyla, 29)

While growing up, I can count the number of times I was held on one hand. Recently my folks were visiting me and I was tearfully explaining how I felt too emotional to go to the site where my brother's ashes were scattered. I sobbingly went to my mother for a comforting hug and was greeted with very stiff arms and great distance between us. (Marguerite, 51)

My relationship with God is the most important part of my life. I feel very close to Him and have complete faith in Him. When I am afraid or scared I know He is there and I feel held and cared for. (Isabelle, 23)

Holding is something that was seldom done in my family by anyone. There was very little physical contact in my family of any nature, not even between my parents. Practically the only way my brother and I were touched was by hitting each other ... at least we got some physical contact that way. (Tina, 40)

I have a sense that my mother was not held very well herself and therefore was not able to hold me very well either. I am not comfortable being held. While I desperately want someone there to hold me, sometimes it is difficult for me to allow myself to be held. I prefer to do the holding for someone else. Holding makes you so dependent on other people, and that is a scary place to be. Being held gives someone the opportunity to drop you. (Wendellyn, 20)

My first significant memory of being held by my father was when I was in the hospital. The nurse had to change my sheets, so I got to sit on my dad's lap. I felt like it had been an eternity since he had his arms around me. I will never forget that feeling of being safe, warm and protected. (Talia, 27)

Finally on June 28th of my senior year I found my real home, Al Anon. That is where I am loved and held. Today I am learning that I can hold myself, and do for myself what others will not do for me. (Winter, 19)

"The most important thing a father can do for his children is to love their mother."

—Theodore Hesburgh

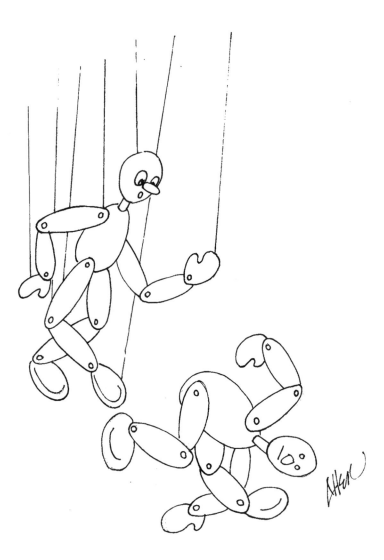

Maybe a relationship with no strings
attached isn't such a good idea.

Chapter 6

Connecting and Attaching

"The meeting of two personalities is like the contact of two chemical substances: if there is any reaction, both are transformed."

—Carl Jung

Taking the risk of attaching to another is a healthy and normal process that contributes deeply to our selfhood, and eventually also causes us great pain. The process of attachment begins in childhood and continues on as we age, providing us ways to learn about others and ourselves with each connection that we make.

We go through our life experiences looking for and enjoying people that we connect with. We connect because we have something in common with them or they seem responsive to us in some way.

Many of us who are animal lovers connect with our pets and with other people's pets because they respond to us. Strange isn't it that it is not a transferable connection? Pets bond with their owners. A pet may be friendly to others, but the exclusivity of the attachment to the owner cannot be overlooked.

A friend of mine will move to Europe and is looking for a new home for her poodle. On the surface, this seems to be a simple task. The dog is cute, well mannered and house broken. But just under the surface is the dog's exclusive connection to her owner.

Left to visit in a new home or left with a dog sitter, the dog is visibly depressed, lethargic and despondent until her owner returns. With her owner in sight, her life spirit returns and she is animated and energetic. She will accept no substitute for her owner except on a temporary basis—and that she accepts grudgingly.

As humans, we also connect and attach in an exclusive manner to the people we select. While we are capable of many attachments and degrees of attachment, the exclusive ones are not transferable.

Suffice it to say that children are not interchangeable. Mates are not interchangeable. Best friends are not interchangeable. We select. We invest in the relationship. We expect over time that the connection will last. In healthy relationships, they do. There is no worse pain than the disappointment or loss of such a connection.

Parents are not interchangeable either, although in today's culture, stepparents are frequently a part of children's lives. Children resist the change and have difficulties accepting the substitute or additional parent figure in their family.

The intensity of this connection speaks to attachment. Attachment is something we do and something we deeply need in our lives. It is not just about our survival as perhaps holding is. It is about the richness of our reality.

Healthy attachment is co-created. Both parties contribute to the meaning and to the experience. It cannot be created alone. The poodle and the owner, the child and the mother, the best friends—all are partners in the attachment relationship.

Attachment is different from holding.

What is attachment? It is remembered feelings and warmth, a primary need and emotional belonging with someone else. Attachment is an active thing we do, in contrast to holding where *they* hold us. We now choose them and hold onto them and that connection is what keeps us from feeling alone. We have a sense of there-ness. If they are there for us, then we don't feel alone; we have a linkage with them. The secure attachment is not so likely to be demonstrated in behavior as much as it is in how we feel inside, which is what determines our connection.

We choose the people we attach to and we won't accept replacements. Interestingly enough, we can be assigned to *hold* someone else but we do not accept the assignment to *attach* to someone else. If you were attached to Dorothy and she wasn't here, I might ask, "Why don't you just attach to Barbara?" You would refuse because it simply doesn't happen that way. Replacing attachments is difficult, because **we choose** whom we attach to. We choose even as infants and children. We don't always choose wisely but, nevertheless, we choose who we will feel close to. Before we've done a lot of thinking, we emotionally link to someone else.

Walking across a college campus, I noticed two guys who were looking at a girl. One of them nudged his friend and said, "I think I'm falling in love." No doubt you've heard that kind of conversation.

However, I've never heard anyone say, "I think I'm falling into attachment." Attachment happens over time; I choose who I attach to and it develops over time. In fact, we cannot fall into attachment. Attachment is probably the most profound of the human experiences—and it involves the deepest feelings.

We feel good when we're around the person we're attached to. We can feel that our gut has been kicked when they are gone. This is the result of attachment; it's an inner sense that we have other people in our world who are special to us—we are not alone.

We need to belong and to feel connected. The people I'm attached to, and the people you're attached to, are like a hub around which our lives revolve. It is the attachments that keep us connected, no matter what else is going on. They don't have to be physically present. You can be sitting where you are now and feel attached to someone who is out there somewhere, even in another country.

Characteristics of Attachment

The characteristics of attachment include the security of predictable responses, intense emotions, emotional belongingness and responsiveness—a history over time—all of which are important.

There are two other often misunderstood characteristics that I would like to emphasize.

1. Attachment passes by unnoticed; we don't notice it until it's gone. We don't realize how attached we are until the person is gone... so go away and I'll tell you if I'm attached to you! "How can I miss you if you won't go away?" is the title of a great country western song.

2. The relationship is taken for granted. I'm so used to you that I don't even notice you anymore. I may not think I'm attached to you.

Perhaps you were not as attached as you thought you were. For example, you believed that you were casual friends with someone who then moved away. The next thing you knew you were feeling sick to your stomach. You felt sharp pains. This came as a surprise, and you asked, "What is this feeling?" You took them for granted and you didn't notice your deep connection. You were surprised to miss them.

The Bird Story

I used to have a cockatiel named Norco. Although I really didn't want the bird, he was given to me. I was not attached to this bird. We coexisted for about twelve years.

One day as I was leaving for work, I looked over at him and he didn't look so good. I scooped him up, took him to the vet and said, "He is not doing well. Would you please fix him and

I'll pick him up after work?"

About an hour later, they called me at work and agreed he didn't look good, and said they would do the best they could. Another hour later, they called back and said they were really sorry, but the bird died. They tried to resuscitate him, but he died. I thanked them for trying and said I would come in and pick up the cage. I felt sad, but it was okay because I wasn't attached to Norco.

I went about my business day and attended a meeting with some of my colleagues. I was sitting in the meeting and the next thing I knew, I burst into tears. Everyone asked what was wrong, and I told them my bird died. They didn't know I had a bird. I wasn't attached. But my tears kept coming so they sent me home.

I went home and called a friend to tell her my bird died, and she reminded me that I wasn't attached. I said, "Yeah, but I just didn't expect this." I asked her to go with me to pick up the cage. I just couldn't face it alone.

We got the cage and brought it back (which I didn't need since there was no bird), but I looked at this empty cage and my heart hurt. Where did he go? What happened? Oh well, he's just a bird, and I'm not attached, I told myself.

The next day wasn't much better. I wasn't quite hysterical but was still upset. I was talking to myself about the fact that I'm a counselor and I should be able to get over this. Besides, I was not attached to the bird. (DENIAL is not just a river in Egypt!) I had the weekend to recover and worked at adjusting to a loss that I did not anticipate.

Some weeks later, my brother visited and took me to a local bird show to see beautiful birds. We saw a cage filled with a lot of Norcos in it. The bird owner asked me if I'd ever had a cockatiel, to which I answered yes. He asked me how long I had had it, at which point I broke down sobbing once again, saying I was attached, but hadn't thought so. Now, I know it's not cool as an adult to break down in public and this response was surprising and embarrassing to me.

My brother was a wise man so he said "pick a new one." I said I didn't want one, then quickly changed my mind and picked one. He got a little cage; we took it home and I felt better. BUT, I was NOT ATTACHED to that bird!

Before you just label me weird, I want you to remember the reason for this story: There are two misunderstood characteristics of attachment:

1. I took the bird for granted, and

2. I didn't know how attached I was until he was gone.

Being attached to someone gives us a sense of belongingness, it's an active process and we hold on in some way to that attachment figure, and these connections continue over time.

Rituals

Most attachment relationships develop some kind of ritual. *A ritual is something that happens frequently and regularly.* I don't know about you but when the phone rings at home, I always look at my watch first to see who it is. If it's a certain time, certain people call. Other times, I'll look at my watch and wonder who it could be, because it's at a time when I'm not used to receiving calls.

When I visited my mother, I noticed that there was a certain time of day when her friend Hattie called for her two-minute chat. She didn't let my mother say a word. Mother just said "hello" and listened until Hattie hung up. I would say, "that was Hattie," and she would reply, "of course." She always knew that was the time when Hattie called. This was their ritual.

Perhaps you have a ritual of getting together for birthdays, or every Friday you meet for coffee, or go walking, go to lunch, visit a thrift shop Saturday mornings, or catch up and touch base with a friend after class. These rituals keep attachment alive.

Identifying Your Rituals

Think about what routines you have that include others. Maybe you call a friend or relative once a month and next month they call you. But you have worked out a routine. When we have an attachment figure, we have some kind of routine with them—a way that we keep that attachment alive. Another point is that rituals are stimulating and sustaining. When we respond in some way to each other, it keeps the relationship going.

Any response, notice the word *any*, (some, a little bit, barely) sustains or continues an existing attachment. Any response works, except neglect.

Attachment Behavior

The experience that we have with our earliest attachment figure becomes a working model for us as to how we expect others to treat us. That's heavy!

What is a model? A replica or a pattern is usually a miniature of the original or the thing which is to be built. When we think of our very first experience of attachment, it can become a pattern of that connection which is to be reproduced for the rest of our lives. A model, a beginning, a replica, and a pattern can become a set of expectations.

If I had great attachments and I was held enough, then my expectations are positive. If I was not held good enough and my early attachments were poor, then what I expect from the world is that attachments are not going to be lasting and fulfilling and they probably are going to be a bad experience. If I attach, I believe that I'm going to get hurt! As a result, I protect myself from what I fear might happen and just don't attach. Even if I'm in a relationship, I tend to keep my attachment feelings guarded. The bottom line is: were people there for you and were they responsive to your needs?

An interesting study, based on J. Bowlby's theory of attachment, observed children when the mother re-entered the room after having dropped them off for a while. When the mother returned to the room, observers noticed how the child responded, and from that they were able to draw some conclusions.

Based on how the child behaved when the mother came back into the room, predictions were made as to how this child might behave in adolescence, in school and as an adult. These are stereotypes to use as starting areas for discussion of how and why we attach or don't attach to the people in our lives.

Let's look at Bowlby's model. A stereotype or model is really just a starting point. We make some guesses. It's a beginning from which we can learn more. The following is a discussion of the model that includes the categories of the secure child, the anxious ambivalent child and the anxious avoidant child.

The summary chart on page 91 shows the three categories of attachment behavior. Along the top of the sheet, you'll get clues as to why a person tends to be in one of these three categories and how these people might behave.

The Impact of Attachment Behavior

The **Secure Child** is secure because they have a consistently responsive and available early attachment figure. In short, their parents were there for them!

A secure child can let you know what they are feeling or thinking directly. If they are under stress or feeling negative, they let you know that. If they are feeling good, they let you know that. They are in touch with their feelings because their first attachment figure was reliable and consistent.

The secure child has access to their feelings. They have thought about their feelings, they can handle them, and they are available, predictable and responsive to others and expect you to be the same with them.

The **Anxious/Ambivalent Child** is very unsure of herself and is dealing with the experiences with their earliest attachment figure who was sometimes responsive and sometimes distant. Sometimes the parents are loving and cozy and cuddly, other times their response to the child is "get away from me." This is crazy making to a child.

This is common in a home where an alcoholic lives because an alcoholic may have two distinct personalities — one when sober and one when drinking. At one time, maybe she is responsive to you and the next time you don't know what will happen. Is she going to behave this way or that way?

The other possible cause with the anxious ambivalent child is that there is a case of role reversal. The adult expects the child to take care of him, instead of the other way around. When that happens, you have more crazy making because the adult unpredictably switches back and forth between the roles. For example, the alcoholic parent asserts, "I'm the father, and that's what I said, and you will do what I told you to do. After all, I'm the father." This is followed by a different persona when the father has been drinking and he says, "I don't feel good, please take care of me."

As an anxious/ambivalent child, it's not safe to express feelings. As a high school student and continuing into college they are preoccupied with relationships. They are always searching for someone to be there. They are really concerned about friendships and relationships, and if they don't have someone to have lunch with, the day is dead. They have got to *have* somebody and don't always trust, if they do have someone, that it's going to last. They are always preoccupied with attachments. They avoid taking a chance expressing feelings because if they do, they don't know what will happen — better to play it cool.

A relationship with an anxious ambivalent often feels smothering.

The **Anxious/Avoidant Child** was always rejected and disappointed by the earliest attachment figure. Why is the anxious/avoidant, anxious and avoidant? He was let down, wounded, had a non-responsive attachment figure and was consistently rejected and disappointed. Promises were made and then consistently broken. People in this category build walls around themselves. They avoid attachment, are self-reliant, hostile and anti-social. They isolate from others.

As a child, the anxious/avoidant has all these sad and hurt feelings which in more adult language might be expressed, "I wish my first attachment figure could be responsive and available to me."

All this disappointment and rejection culminates in the erroneous conclusion that there is something wrong with **me**, because this significant other person (Dad, Mom, Sister, or Brother) consistently disappointed or rejected me. All that added up brings the emotional conclusion that "people can't be trusted—therefore I will never, never risk trusting again." It all begins with the feeling of being emotionally wounded.

The anthem of the anxious avoidant is "I don't do relationships." They might say, "You know what, I don't do relationships. I tell you that but you don't believe me. I don't want them. You may need them, but I don't." My advice? Believe them! They are telling you their truth. Believe them.

Check out the following chart that shows some of the characteristics for each type.

Working Models of Attachment

	Secure Children Responsive, available attachment figure; good enough parent.	Anxious Ambivalent Sometimes responsive, sometimes distant; often alcoholic/addicted parent.	Anxious Avoidant Rejected, disappointed; consistently disappointed by parent.
Child to Age 6	Secure children protest the mother's absences, but remain confident that she will return, and they greet her enthusiastically.	Uncertain about the responsiveness and availability of the mother, and they treat her ambivalently when reunited with her.	Do not have confidence in their mother's responsiveness and don't seek her out or greet her on return—try not to need her.
School Age	Self-reliant, emotionally open, able to manage and express feelings.	Avoid the expression of feelings, responds with passivity or disorganization. (Child often parents the parent.)	Bullying and other anti-social behaviors.
Adolescence	Likely to be competent and venturesome in the struggle for identity. Work to maintain their self.	Preoccupied, most anxious about attachments, feels less competent, always very concerned about relationships.	Believe relationships to be distant and unsupportive. Do not trust that others will be there for them.
College Students	Able to balance negative feelings even under stress; less anxious and more socially competent.	Same as above in Adolescence	Relationships are distant and unsupportive. Compulsively self-reliant.
Adults	Emotionally available, predictable, and responsive and expect others to be the same.	Anxious about attachment, perhaps even preoccupied with it, always fearful of abandonment, always searching for someone to be there. Need to learn to be there for themselves.	Screen out awareness of attachment issues. Try to rely only on self. "They don't do relationships" (believe them). Major trust issues.

91

Connecting and Attaching

Connections

There are different kinds of connections. If you get involved with someone who does crazy making stuff, you're going to behave in a crazy manner. That's what crazy making is designed to do. Our attachment type perpetuates the same behavior.

You're going to respond to type. If you are with a secure person, you get to be secure. It IS a transferable trait! When we feel that we are worthy of someone who is predictable, reliable and responsible, then that's what we hold out for in a relationship.

If you are with an anxious/ambivalent person, you may start behaving in that preoccupied insecure way. If you are with someone who always disappoints or rejects you, then you will see the world as a place that disappoints and rejects and is not to be trusted.

When you hear yourself say, "That person is my type," ask yourself, "What is my type? What is my habit? What is familiar? What am I going to do with this?"

If you are with someone who is hurting you, you might begin to close off parts of yourself in order to protect yourself. When you begin to close off parts of your emotions, pretty soon you may close down all of them.

Of utmost importance when selecting a friend, a colleague, a partner, a boyfriend or a girlfriend is to **CHOOSE THAT SOMEBODY CAREFULLY**. Choose someone you can count on—right from the beginning. You probably see people more clearly when you first meet them than you ever see them again. You see the characteristics that bother you. If you tend to forgive these traits right away or pretend that you don't see them, you invite people into your life that may frustrate or hurt you.

Think about the impact other people have on you. Other people modify your behavior. You modify theirs.

When you ask someone to hold you, it's because you believe

they are strong enough to do so. However, you can become attached to someone who is considerably weaker than you are. One of the most seductive things anyone can say to you is: I NEED YOU!

In a healthy relationship both people need each other —interdependently.

Tens and Zeros

Some connections are built on an unequal status or power basis. They can be deep attachments that are not necessarily healthy. For example, if one person is very needy and the other is the rescuer or the controlling one, what we have is a Zero and a Ten. While all of us can be in need at sometimes, we try in relationships to be balanced and to interchange the times of being needy and the times of giving back to the other person.

There are some people in life who in order to feel like a Ten keep a Zero around. It has to do with control issues. It's not about strength or health or how talented you are. In a sense they'll hire you: "How would you like to be my Zero?" I will treat you, pay the bills, I will give you spending money, be nice to you sometimes and let you go to the mall on Saturday. The only thing you have to agree to is to be a Zero to my Ten. You will be under my control."

One day Zero says that this has been okay for a while, but now I'd like to be a real person. The Ten responds, "No, no. The deal is you're the Zero and I'm the Ten." If Zero decides to become a Five, Ten will work on them until they become a Zero again. The rule is, "Thou shalt not grow!"

*Tens can be abusive. "Don't you remember you're nothing without me? You won't even be that much when you leave because no one else will have you." There are all kinds of words of harassment Ten will use to keep that person as a Zero.

*(F.Y.I. If your situation becomes violent, the National Domestic Violence Hotline is 1-800-799-Safe [7233])

If Zero reaches a point where they decide, "I don't like this — I'm outta here," and they leave, the Ten will go out and find another Zero. Ten doesn't want to be in an equal relationship, and Ten doesn't believe the other person can be an equal. To be healthy, the Zero will have to leave that relationship and learn to grow. The Zero will then have the opportunity to find someone who chooses healthy togetherness where both persons get to be Tens.

Whether the attachment is healthy or not healthy, it is always about deep feelings.

To be attached to someone is a profound and deep experience. To have an ending to that attachment can be profoundly painful.

Breaking Up or Ending an Attachment Relationship

Many people who are trying to break off a relationship say to each other, "It's over." One wants it, the other doesn't, and at some point they come to the conclusion that they are breaking up.

One might say, "I don't think this is working so I think we should just be friends." Unfortunately, being friends doesn't work for a while since the other person is bleeding emotionally (assuming that they didn't want the break up). While the goal of friendship after a break up is a good one in theory, it must be postponed for at least two years in order to allow emotional healing.

When you are in that process, the kindest thing you can do is to say, "I'm not going to be seeing, calling or talking to you, or being with you for a while." This is a kindness because any contact continues the attachment feelings.

After some time passes, perhaps the breaker-upper calls the breakupee to ask, "How are you doing?" Ouch! As soon as you call them, the breakupee feels renewed pain. They might even think there is HOPE. The breaker-upper would do better to leave them alone. Remember that any contact will continue that attachment.

Let's say I go through a horrendous break up and I'm getting better and I decide I'm strong enough to call him up and make some kind of contact. We talk, and then I receive the following letter:

Dear Jan,

I hate you. I don't like you. I don't ever want to see you again. Don't call, don't think about me and don't come by. Never, never, never do I want to see you again—you're an awful person.

George

I look at the note and might erroneously think, "See, he still cares because he took the time to write." ANY RESPONSE encourages. So I think somehow he does care. Yes, there is an error in my thinking, but that's what I want to think. That's how the attachment is sustained. Ridiculous? But haven't you seen this or felt this yourself?

After a break up, the next step is to agree we're not going to see each other or connect in any way. Otherwise, it's going to keep the wound open. Let me use an example about physical healing. I sliced my leg open and went to the doctor and he sewed it up with stitches. A couple of weeks later I was feeling better and thought it must be healed. I wanted to see how much it had healed, so I reached down and spread the stitches apart to look inside.

Does that make any sense? You may think that is ridiculous but when we have contact with someone we are trying to get over, we literally reopen the emotional wound. It's important if you're the breaker-upper to be kind to your ex and leave them alone. If you're the breakupee, then take care of yourself and stay away from your ex.

Any contact is going to keep that wound open. Any response from them perpetuates an existing attachment; that is, ANY RESPONSE EXCEPT total NEGLECT. So neglect during a break up is a good thing!

Like the Air We Breathe

We need to have attachment figures. We are built to attach to others, the same way we are built to breathe. We need them and they need us. This is a human developmental expression. Not to have people in our lives is to be tremendously alone—to feel tremendous pain.

In Ruthellen Josselson's book, *The Space Between Us*, she asserts, "Attachment is a biologically and ethologically routed system not necessarily cognitively explainable."

Wouldn't that make a great valentine card? "I am biologically and ethologically drawn to you in a way that I can't cognitively explain!"

When your mother or father asks why are you attached to that person or what you see in that boyfriend or girlfriend, wouldn't it be wonderful to say, "It is a biologically and ethologically routed system not necessarily cognitively explainable." Memorize this if you love a playful answer!

We all know what biologically means, but what does ethologically mean? It refers to animal behavior; it's normal, natural and the way we are. We are built that way—to breathe, and to attach. *It's not necessarily cognitively explainable* means I cannot explain it to you from my head because I am linking from my feelings. Attachment is about feelings, deep feelings.

When we consider how fast our world is moving and all the changes that we're dealing with—we're highly mobile, highly fluid—there is a lot of disconnecting in modern life. So our attachments keep us connected.

How many people are you still in touch with that go back to your high school days? I remember our senior class president in high school saying at the final graduation banquet, "Look around now at the people you have seen daily for years, and think about the fact that you may never see them again." That comment has stayed with me! I never did see them again.

Friends form the continuity. Friends over time are continually responsive and are the persons that we can count on.

An attachment relationship can be with our mother, father, sister, brother, aunt, cousin, best friend, colleague, mate, neighbor or anyone who is special to us.

There are a lot of different levels of attachment; we can have a mini attachment or a major attachment. A mini attachment, for example, is when I go to work everyday and at the front desk the two people sitting there smile and welcome me. That to me is responsive, and it is continuing—all the time. It's not like one day they growl at me and the next they are kind. They always say, "Hi, Jan." That's it. I don't see them on the weekend, outside of work. But there is an attachment because there is a link. You have that in your workplace, at your place of worship or in your neighborhood. Maybe all you do is say, "Hi, Neighbor." But that is a mini link and you look forward to that. There are other neighbors you don't speak to at all.

A major attachment is with a mate, family, dear friends, puppies, and kitties, and we become anxious or worried about attachments if there is some kind of threat that the relationship might not be there or continue.

Attachment is a tremendously profound emotion, an essential element of growing and developing as a person.

ACTION ITEM ··········▶

Mapping Your Relationships

Return to your relationship maps that you created in Chapter 1. Use an A to mark on your maps those with whom you feel you have an attachment.

Questions to ponder

As you think about these people, and answer the following questions, write your thoughts in your journal.

- ▶ Who are my major attachments that have lasted over time?
- ▶ Who is important to me that I may be taking for granted?
- ▶ What attachments do I need to let go of in order to heal or to grow?
- ▶ Have I told the people who are important to me that I really care for them and appreciate what they bring to my life?

Answering these questions will help you to focus on attachments that have been a significant part of your togetherness that works. It may also give you clues as to how to appreciate and grow the attachments that work and truly let go of those that have hurt you. You can connect and attach differently if that is what you want.

I feel I have nobody to talk to. My parents are alcoholics, I have never gotten along with my sister and I find it hard to fully trust my friends. I find myself saying that I don't need anybody. I believe in that, but I know I need someone. My very best friend right now is my dog, but my goal is to find a girlfriend, a companion to share my life with. (Paul, 20)

> My cat (not really a person) is one of the people I'm attached to. I don't seem to care about her, but when she's not around I miss her. I am one of those people who would say, "I am not attached," but when the day comes when the cat is gone, I would go nuts. (Adam, 21)

I now realize that getting attached to someone without knowing them is very dangerous, both emotionally and physically. (Toni, 26)

> Maybe I just hopelessly needed other people in my life, and when the feeling of being needed didn't come from my family I searched elsewhere. (Deanne, 22)

My heart sunk when I heard that I would have to go two years with no contact at all before I'd be ready to be friends with my ex. It made a lot of sense though, so I took a deep breath and thought, Well, I have two days done already. That just leaves me one year and 363 days to go! (Noreen, 55)

> "Friendship is born at that moment when one person says to another: 'What! You, too? Thought I was the only one.'"
>
> —C.S. Lewis

Don't you have anything on improving others?

Chapter 7

The Experience of Loss and the Journey to Healing

"All human life has its seasons and cycles, and no one's personal chaos can be permanent. Winter, after all, gives way to spring and summer, though sometimes when branches stay dark and the earth cracks with ice, one thinks they will never come, that spring, and that summer, but they do and always."

— Truman Capote

Anytime we connect to another human being, we know that at some point we may have to say goodbye to them. Some tips about how to get through the loss along with ways to understand the process of healing will help keep us sane.

A big loss almost always feels like a big surprise. There seems to be no way to prepare for the feelings that come, even when we think we are prepared.

When we experience loss and the feelings that go with it, we come to understand how attached we were to whomever it is we've lost. When we talk about attachment, we have to talk about loss. As stated before, there are some who refuse to attach to anyone or anything because it's too painful. "If I attach, I'm going to lose them. If I attach, eventually it's going to hurt." They avoid any connections and "do not do relationships."

When we lose someone, it's going to hurt. That's true. On the other hand, we get the joy of the attachment relationship while we're in it—and for as long as we're in it. To attach or not to attach—that's a choice we each have to make.

Experiencing loss requires that we go through a process of surviving the loss. It is this process that we want to figure out. What is loss? What does it feel like? Loss is an absence, an ache in the pit of the stomach, a sense of the whole body shaking like an earthquake, a sense of disbelief and despair, a sense of being lost and empty. Sometimes it's a feeling of panic, paralysis and numbness. The depth of it seems to be directly proportionate to the depth of connection we had with the person. It can shake a person to the core of their being and change them forever.

As we go through the grieving process, it feels like we have dropped into a bottomless pit and are going to stay there forever.

We change. If we understand a little about the process, we still feel the pain intensely, but at least we know where we are in that process, and there may be comfort in that. When it comes to understanding loss and the grieving process, we have been blessed with the work of Elizabeth Kubler-Ross, who has worked with terminally ill adults and children with AIDS, and who has written books on death and dying to help us understand the grieving process. She says there are six stages to our grieving in much the same way that there are stages when we heal from a physical injury.

Physical Healing

Take a look at the physical healing process. Have you ever broken a bone and needed to wear a cast? When you have something that's broken, what's the process? It swells up and hurts. The doctor puts a cast on it. While you have the cast on, it begins to itch. You go back to the doctor and tell her it's itch-ing and she says, "Good, you're healing." It's part of the process: you ache, you get upset, it takes time, it throbs, it itches, it gets better and you go on with your life.

When we have a cast on, people give us sympathy and ask, "What happened to you?" However, emotional hurting is not visible. We don't wear a cast around our heart that says our heart is broken. While our friends don't see an obvious outward sign of our injury/pain, we still must go through these stages of healing, which are painful but predictable.

Let's look at the stages of emotional grieving we all go through when we get bad news or suffer a terrible loss.

- Denial: NO WAY, it didn't happen. That's our first reaction.
- Anger: Lashing out, boiling, this is not what I wanted; it's not fair.
- Bargaining: Let's make a deal.
- Depression: Rocky Road ice cream, PJs and TV, plus lots of tears.
- Acceptance: So, this is the way it's going to be, huh?
- Healing and Hope: While I don't like this, I can go on now.

If we experience a minor loss, we may go through this process very quickly. If, however, we experience a major loss, then we will go through a transition that usually lasts from one to three years. Yes, one to three years. This is the process. For this amount of time we work our way through these stages.

Here's an example of a minor transition:

I stayed up too late last night. This morning when the alarm went off I thought, "Oh no, it can't be. No way, it cannot be time to get up!" (Denial)

Right after that I thought, "How come I have to get up? Why can't it just be Saturday? There are lots of other people in the world who don't have to get up at this hour. This is the worst!" (Anger)

Then I do something called Bargaining; I hit the "snooze alarm" and buy myself five more minutes of peace. Seconds later, I'm asleep again. Soon the alarm re-rings and I realize, "Oh no, that didn't work."

You can see how the first three stages are designed to make it go away. I've tried to pretend it didn't happen. I've tried to scare it away by being angry, and finally I've tried bargaining to get around it. None of it worked. It still is what it is.

Now I've crossed that line and gone into Depression; "Woe is me, I have to get up and I'm still tired. This is an awful day and morning. I feel awful." The only good news about depression is that we are halfway through the healing process.

Then I get this thought, "Wait a minute, I have to get up, but it's pay day! And I get to meet a friend for lunch. They are always so cheerful and lively; I'm going to feel better—I guess I can deal with that." (Acceptance)

So I get up, and I think, well, I Hope I remember to go to bed earlier tonight.

In this example, I've gone through the stages of grieving in minutes. But for major losses it's different. It can last one to three years. We must be patient with ourselves during this process and also realize that setbacks may occur.

It is important not to get stuck in any of the stages of grieving, but to move through all of them to really heal. Perhaps you know someone who is stuck in depression or anger. The bitterness of staying stuck will consume the person rather than serving them in subsequent life events and future relationships. Sometimes getting help in the form of counseling or joining a grief group will help a person get unstuck.

Understanding the stages of healing allows us to know where we are in a process that makes sense to us, tells us what lies ahead, and that we know works.

A boy wrote the following poem:

The Color Black

Black is a raven that flies in the light.
It's also the charcoal that burns through the night.
Black is a jet that goes zoom, zoom, zoom.
It's also the color of space leaning against the moon.
Black is the color of a bad memory.
It's the color of a cat walking through a cemetery.
Black is the color of darkness that spreads all around.
It's also the color of freshly turned ground.
Black is the color of a broken heart,
When you lose your best friend,
And your world falls apart.

—Dillan Tucker

Dillan was ten and his best friend had to move away and it broke his heart. Can you feel his pain?

The feelings of attachment and connecting with someone and the loss of that connection repeat again and again throughout our lives. Both adults and children feel and experience loss. Many times they deal with it alone. Can you imagine wandering through the experience and the feelings of a major loss without any awareness of the process of healing?

What helps us to feel better? When someone is there for us, we feel safer. We attach to others because it keeps away loneliness. We have a sense that our lives are emotionally linked. Relationships keep us connected. We are not alone.

There are times, as in the death of a loved one, when we know it's a good thing for the person who is gone, even if it's a devastating time for us. We want them back although we're glad, for example, that the person is not suffering anymore, or that they didn't suffer at all. We are glad that an illness was short-term instead of long-term and that the suffering is at an end. Despite the relief for the one who is gone, we may still be in pain. Sometimes we selfishly find it difficult to appreciate the good, even for them.

We suffer because it was a wonderful relationship and sometimes we suffer because it was not a wonderful relationship. We grieve what we missed out on or what might have been, if only they could have been different. We suffer, we feel the loss and we grow from the pain. We learn and we grow... reluctantly.

Relationship Loss

We can lose a partner, a job, our health, a friend, our status, our income, a home in a tragic fire or our faith. We may even grieve the loss of the *potential* of a relationship. We grieve that it never worked out for us.

Along with the grieving and emptiness and the great hole that exists inside a person when a partner dies or leaves, comes the fear that such a relationship might never come along again.

Bizarre and scary questions may surface. We may ask ourselves:

▶ What if my intelligence, my looks, my personality and my desirability all disappear?
▶ What if I don't find a replacement right away?
▶ Do I even want a replacement?
▶ How will I get through this time?
▶ Who am I now?
▶ I have to create a whole new life. How do I do that?

I have to have a relationship may become the desperate theme to help with the healing.

And then follows the fear of, Maybe I've lost what it takes to begin another relationship. Here's an antidote to many of the uncertainties you may be feeling:

● First of all, you do not have to create a whole new life.
● What's ahead is a new chapter, not a new life.

- It is now a matter of building on the old life and adding new chapters to it.

You don't need to get rid of all that you have been for so long. Add parts and pieces to the old chapters.

Build on the "you" from before your loss and the successes that you have enjoyed over your lifetime.

ACTION ITEM ··········▶

Healing Questions

Ask yourself:

▶ Where (in what environment) can I heal the best? (Mountains, ocean, desert, city, etc.)

▶ What short-term experiences can I "try on"? (Take a class, learn a new skill/sport, start working out, take a trip, etc.)

▶ What short-term relationships can I connect with? (Same-gender friends can be a life-saver on Sunday afternoons.)

Make notes in your journal. Remember, these are short-range decisions, not permanent long-term decisions.

Chances are you simply are not ready for long-term commitment thinking or a long-term relationship yet.

The pain you are feeling includes the birthing pains of your new chapter. As you say good-bye to the chapter that has ended, you are getting ready to create a new chapter. Out of the pain of loss will be a new you. Think short-term only. Sometimes, short-term is ten minutes! Do not try to find a long-term new relationship before you know who you are in your next chapter. As you change, you will shop for a different kind of partner. Choosing a person now would be choosing out of pain, not necessarily choosing from your healthiest self.

Some of your coupled friends might find you to be a threat as a single again. Look for opportunities to meet new people.

Perhaps you can organize a group that will have dinner together once a month for awhile.

If you date and are having sex—use a condom! The rule is "No glove, no love." Things are different now with AIDS and other STD's.

If you are in a grief support group—keep that group for support. Therapy can be an intense experience. Keep it separate from dating. Find people to date from a different "activity" group, that is, a hiking group or a bicycle group, or a church group.

Think in terms of short-term employment rather than a full career if this is a time when you need to find new avenues of income. Perhaps take a no-brainer job for a while to have structure, along with some income, but fewer responsibilities.

Give yourself time to deal with the pain of loss. You know the stages of grieving. There is no way to hurry this. If you rush the healing, it won't be honest.

Make a shopping list of characteristics desired in the next partner. Women tend to make character lists like: I want a man who is warm, caring, kind, loving, sensitive and fun. Men tend to make "do-lists" and want a person who can bike, play, go to movies, be fun, likes sex and wants to travel.

The idea is to make the list and then shop (or hang out) where people do the things you like to do. There is no shop for people who are "warm." (Breathing is a characteristic of most humans!) The more specific you are in your list, the more likely you are to find what you really want.

For one woman who said she wanted someone who tried to help others and was an outdoor type, I recommended volunteering with Habitat for Humanity. There are fixers and doers and care type people there! There are groups for just about any interest or activity you can think of. A little research can put you in touch with new people who share your fascination with gray whales, gardening, golf, etc.

Part of planning your next chapter is to include interim experiences so that the pressure of long-term permanent decisions is postponed until you have your feet under you. Interim decisions give you time. Time as part of the healing process allows you clarity and more personal peace. It takes time. Give yourself that time.

One of my favorite Bible verses is: And it came to pass . . ., which translates as, It didn't come to stay. You will feel better. Just don't rush your own expectations. Most of all be patient with yourself. This too shall pass.

Your friends may tire of your healing process long before your healing takes place. Be patient with them too!

Loss hurts. Grieving is a process. You will get through it if you honor the process and take the time you need to heal. This will prepare you for your next chapter. Perhaps the best is yet to come.

ACTION ITEM ·········▶

Journal On!

This is a great time to write in your journal. Write what you are feeling. Don't worry about complete sentences. Just gasp. Write. Don't reread anything you've written. As feelings come up for you, don't judge them. Just say to yourself, isn't that interesting!

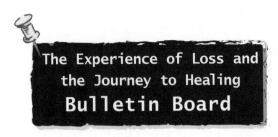

The Experience of Loss and
the Journey to Healing
Bulletin Board

I am at a huge crossroads in my life. My primary relationship over the past several years has been with my son. Now that he is preparing to go out and have his own life away from me, I want to construct a life that will fulfill me and bring me into connection with God, myself and with others who are on a parallel journey to mine. (Donald, 40)

I was surprised how grieving can transpire without actually going through the episode of death. You can experience grief by having a traumatic change in your life. For instance, when I got sober, I had to change people, places and things, and with that change in my life I had felt all the stages of grief: Denial that I had to change my old ways, Angry that I became an addict, Bargaining to make changes so it wouldn't happen again, Depressed that I had to start my life over, Acceptance that my life can get better and is getting better without the use of drugs and alcohol, and finally having hope and healing from the support of my fellowship. Those six stages have helped me understand what I was experiencing when I was feeling all that pain and hurt. (Lena, 31)

I have felt alone much of my life…out of touch…and during the past five years I have experienced a significant amount of loss, including the loss of my mother, followed by the death of my closest high school buddy, and then a close friend. I have also worked a lot with people dying of AIDS and cancer patients and have felt like a part of me has died. I have also lost a part of my career, have moved from Los Angeles, and have lost "my youth" and my naiveté. In some strange way I feel like I lost my childhood. (Isaac, 47)

I feel a sense of loss and miss my little boy and simultaneously I have a new connection to the young man he's becoming. (Ivan, 45)

Who wants to go through the pain and suffering of losing someone after you invested so much time getting attached to them in the first place? Sounds like an investment with absolutely no return. (Melanie, 31)

> Though I now understand that with attachment comes loss, I don't believe that was something I realized when I was four years old and my parents went through a messy divorce. I had lost a father and I had lost a family. After that I found it hard to stay attached to anyone for very long. Then another blow was dealt when my only grandfather died. Till this day he remains my absolute idol; I still miss him and sadly remember the day he left me. I had been there the day he died and had seen him only hours before he died. It was the last time that I really attached myself to anybody, heart and soul. (Celia, 29)

I did not grieve my dad in the usual way. You see, nothing was left unsaid; I had a happy relationship with him for my forty-six years. He held me; I was attached to him in life and remain so in death. I was able to let him pass into the next stage knowing a wonderful peace. He is not far from me. I feel his presence almost palpably. He is only gently passed beyond, not yet deep into eternity. (Eliza, 49)

111

The Experience of Loss

"You went on living one day after another, and in time, you were somebody else, your previous self only like a close relative, a sister or brother, with whom you shared a past, but a different person, a separate life."

—Charles Frazier, from *Cold Mountain*

I could be happy if someone just said that they liked me.

I really don't think I can do that.

Chapter 8

Validating Others and Ourselves

"The first duty of love is to listen." — Paul Tillich

Becoming real to others and ourselves is born in the eye-to-eye connections with our earliest significant others. Without it, we do not exist as a self. When we offer validation to others, we give the greatest gift of all.

The essence of bad validation experiences and good validation experiences is expressed through our eyes and felt in our bones. Even small children sense the human need for and power of eye contact.

- ▶ Can you remember a delightful time when you felt so validated that you were utterly confident?
- ▶ Can you remember a dark time when the lack of validation left you in the emotional dumpster?
- ▶ What did those times look like and how did they feel?
- ▶ Can you believe the power in those experiences?

It's not unusual for a child to be clear about the need for eye contact, particularly when we are busy and we're going about our business or we're reading, washing the dishes, etc. The child reaches over and grabs our cheeks, turns our face toward them and says, "Look at me, Mommy, look at me!" They force us to make eye contact with them because instinctively they know how important that is. They force an interruption for us because they need to matter.

We can see how much we matter to another person when we look into their eyes and they look back; we can see that our existence is, or is not, valued.

And What Is Validation?

We matter to ourselves when we matter to someone else. We tend to value ourselves to the extent that someone else values us. If you value me, I feel valuable. When someone looks at you in an intense loving way, you feel prized, cherished, special and particularized. There is this sense that you *exist*, and that it's a good existence; you are special.

Good validation has a look to it that we recognize. First of all, we know that the giver means what they say and that the feedback is real. It is mostly nonverbal. It is recognizable in smiles, eye contact and respect. We have the sense that the one validating is paying attention to us and is willing to interrupt what they are doing to make time for us. We feel listened to and heard. We feel good about ourselves in their presence, and we feel appreciated.

One of the most vivid examples of eye-to-eye validation can be experienced any day of the week in the arrivals area of any airport. Along with hundreds of other people getting off the plane, you may pass by masses of people waiting for their loved ones and remain totally indifferent to them, when all of a sudden you see the person you are looking for. You make eye contact and your face lights up! So does theirs. The rest of the people disappear. This is the validation moment. I see you, you see me, no one else is important. It doesn't matter to me how many other people are there, and for the person looking for me, the hundreds of other people don't matter either. When we get that kind of eye contact we know we have been recognized, but also that we exist for that other person in a very special way.

In contrast, if a significant person doesn't value me, and

puts me down as if I don't matter, then I have trouble valuing myself. Put-downs contain hurtful words and hurtful looks. We can feel "diss-ed", dismissed, disregarded, discouraged, disbelieved, disgust from the speaker and ignored. There can be condescension in their voice and we in turn feel a sense of rejection, isolation and loneliness.

What Is Personal Validation?

The idea of validation in our case is that someone else, when they look into our eyes, can authenticate us, can give us value. We exist when someone looks into our eyes. We are acknowledged as being present; we are THERE.

The validation issue is as simple as this: **You were or you were not valued. You were or you were not validated. Everything stems from that—your issues, your self doubts, your confidence and your fears. Everything stems from your validation history.**

I am not what you think I am,
And I am not what I think I am;
I am (or I become), what I think you think I am.
(Read those three lines again!)

Becoming Real

Even before we can discuss the implications of validation, we must talk about a mother's experience with her newborn infant. How many new mothers and new fathers have been amazed that in the moments just after birth, the newly arrived infant searches out the eyes of its mother? The profound eye-to-eye moment connects that mother and child and tips the scale in favor of that baby's survival. The infant needs that eye contact to exist as a self.

When we are acknowledged and affirmed that we are really here, that sense is always in the eyes. As an infant, I become *real* when someone lets me know that I'm real in their eyes. They look at me! They really look at me!

We all know that at night when we go to sleep our toys talk to each other. Margery Williams's wonderful book, *The Velveteen Rabbit*, is about toys who talk to each other; the biggest, oldest, and wisest of them is the Skinhorse.

The Skinhorse had lived longer in the nursery than any of the others. He was so old that his brown coat was bald in patches and showed the seams underneath, and most of the hairs in his tail had been pulled out to string bead necklaces. He was wise, for he had seen a long succession of mechanical toys arrive to boast and swagger and by and by break their main springs and pass away. He knew that they were only toys and would never turn into anything else.

Nursery magic is very strange and wonderful and only those play things that are old and wise and experienced like the Skinhorse understand all about it.

"What is real?" asked the rabbit one day when they were lying side by side in the nursery. Does it mean having things that buzz inside you and a stick-out handle?

"Real isn't how you are made," said the Skinhorse, "it's a thing that happens to you. When a child loves you for a long, long time—not just to play with—but really loves you, then you become real."

"Does it hurt?" asked the rabbit.

"Sometimes," said the Skinhorse, for he was always truthful. "When you are real, you don't mind being hurt."

"Does it happen all at once like being wound up or bit-by-bit?" he asked.

"It doesn't happen all at once," said the Skinhorse. "You become. It takes a long time. That's why it doesn't happen to people who break easily, or have sharp edges or have to be carefully kept. Generally, by the time you are real, most of your hair has been loved off, your eyes drop out and you get loose in the joints, and you get very shabby. But these things don't matter at all, because once you are "real" you can't be ugly, except to people who don't understand."

"I suppose you are real," said the rabbit. Then he wished he hadn't said it because he thought the Skinhorse might be sensitive. But the Skinhorse only smiled. "The boy's uncle made me real, and that was many years ago. But once you are real, you can't become unreal again — it lasts for always."

Once we get this validation, this proof that we are real, we "can't become unreal again—it lasts for always."

This is validation; this is becoming REAL.

When There Is Lack of Support

In contrast to feeling real, have you ever gotten the silent treatment from someone? This is when a person looks through you as if you aren't there. What does that feel like? Like you're not there, rejection, there's no value to the experience, you're nothing, you don't exist — it's not a good feeling. So much of messaging comes from the eyes.

A successful actress confessed to a TV interviewer that she had severe stage fright, to the degree that at times she couldn't perform. The idea of eye-to-eye validation came to my mind when she spoke of having a mother who didn't approve of her, and a stepfather who refused to look at her. This woman is a producer, a singer, an actress and an individualist. She has made millions of dollars as a celebrity. Yet here is a person with all of these accolades and she has stage fright, and she says her stepfather refused to look at her when she talked, or even when she performed. He refused to validate her.

There are fans that look at her adoringly, applaud, cheer and throw money at her because she's so talented. Even with all these people looking at her, she says she has stage fright. I thought to myself, why don't all these millions of people matter? Even when she's being validated by her fans, it's not what she wanted. She wanted attention from her parents. She finally grew in her own self and said, in effect, "It would be really nice if they paid attention to me, but you know what, I've moved on."

Now what about you? Is there someone whose approval you want to have who continually refuses to give it to you? You may be intent on getting that one person to notice you. You do all kinds of things just to get attention from that one person. Perhaps they are unwilling or unable to give that to you. Either way, you don't get the attention that you desire.

Well, take a look around! Maybe you don't have millions of people applauding and cheering and wanting your autograph, but do you notice that your best friend, your mate, your child, your neighbor, or your colleagues are saying, "Good job!" You don't let it count because you're choosing to focus on the one person from whom you want validation. You've picked this particular person to provide the only validation that matters to you. And you discount all others. By ignoring them you lose.

By continually going back to that person for validation even though they don't give it, you'll keep getting hurt over and over. You don't have to stay stuck in this routine. You have a choice: you can continue to seek that validation from the special someone who doesn't give it or you can fire him or her, and get it from someone else. That's the secret: You can unpick!

Subconsciously we don't always know that. But it is true. We can unpick and repick.

Gravel Friends versus Birdseed Friends

We grow only with the help of interpersonal nutrients. Nutrients are the things that sustain us — like food, vitamins or minerals. We ingest nutrients in order to grow and in order to be healthy. If we have a houseplant that we simply water and nothing else, pretty soon it turns yellow, pale. It isn't growing because it needs nutrients in addition to water.

To illustrate, I'll share another Norco story. I was going to be away for several days so I asked my neighbor to come in and feed my bird Norco while I was gone. She agreed. I told her that the birdseed was on the countertop.

When I returned and looked at Norco, he was sitting there, looking up at me, and making a pitiful sound. When I looked in the seed cup, it was filled with gravel! I was really shocked by this, and dumped the gravel out. There were two bags on the counter, one bag of birdseed and one bag of gravel. My neighbor had inadvertently filled the birdseed cup with gravel. She chose not to look into the other bag. Looking further would have provided nutrients.

I filled the cup with seed and Norco ate, and ate and ate and finally came up for air as if to say thank you. I thought about how anyone could mistake gravel for birdseed. This was beyond me. But apparently it is possible to confuse birdseed nourishment with hard cold gravel.

Now you may think that it's a sad person who mistakes gravel for birdseed but let me ask you something. Do you have gravel friends? Do you have friends or members of your family who take energy away from you but give little or nothing back? Gravel friends have no nutritional benefits. Actually, some so-called friends may not be just gravel or lacking nutrients. They may even be toxic! Toxic people are poisonous to us and to our sense of self.

People in our lives have to be nutritious in order for us to grow. If you have gravel friends, dump them and get some birdseed friends! If they are gravel friends, they are not giving you any nourishment! There are no nutrients in gravel.

When we have people in our lives that don't nourish us, our *self* doesn't grow, anymore than my bird Norco could grow or even live much longer on gravel. As human beings, we make allowances, we adapt to people who are not nourishing us, erroneously thinking they probably need us more than we need them. Either that or we'll stay in a relationship because, after all, we are used to them. And we stay even though we don't receive any nutrients.

How do you identify a gravel friend? One clue is when you notice that you are with someone who ALWAYS drains you. Then you may be in the gravel friend zone. If they don't have any emotional resources for themselves, they don't have any to give to you. May I suggest that you begin to limit the time with them and begin to replace them with someone who is nutritious for you?

I repeat, if you have gravel friends, dump them and get some birdseed friends to add nourishment to your life.

Validation never comes from someone who doesn't have any nutrients to give, or who doesn't choose to share them. You need to be less and less available to those people. If you want to keep them in your life you can — it's your choice — but make sure you've got a balance of people who have something to offer to your growth!

In our society, we're taught that we have to be our own person — we need to have a self, which resides in us. What's important to remember is that self is connected to other people too. It's part of our growing process as human beings. As humans we are held, we learn to connect with others, we are touched, and the next step is to exist as a self and that requires eye-to-eye validation. Over the course of our lifetime, we need to be validated. It's a combination of "Yes, I have to be strong in myself", but also, "I have to have some validating voices to feed and nurture my self."

We need to have positive voices in our lives to remind us of who we are, that we exist. It's why we all need good friends, family, extended family, and others in our lives. Feeling "real" is more than just existing; it is finding a way to exist as one's self, and to continue to relate to others as that self. More importantly, a well-defined 'self' becomes a safe harbor in which we rest and restore.

Mentoring and Validation

This is another part of validation. We need someone to confirm the self that we are becoming, when we are not sure who we are yet. If we're lucky enough, we may find a mentor, someone who knows who we are and what we might become.

A mentor sees the potential in us that we don't see in ourselves yet. We may focus on our limits, unable to project into the future the way another person can for us. When a teacher, guide or mentor sees us as we might someday be, we are given the gift of believing we can do something that we haven't considered. Who do you have in your life that mentors you? Who do you mentor?

Perhaps you are afraid of taking a risk of some kind and simply need a boost or a vote of confidence from someone. This kind of validation is one of the most important parts of parenting, teaching and mentoring.

When a coach says, "You can do it. I'm counting on you," you reach down and pull up the confidence to do something that maybe you don't quite believe you can do. When a coach sees that ability in you, you begin to believe it too!

How someone else sees us affects our own reality. *If you believe in me, then I can be more than what I thought I could be.*

Unfortunately, the opposite is also true. *If you think I'm going to be less than I think I can be, you may discourage me to the point where I don't try.*

Has that happened to you? Have you had things you wanted to do but became discouraged when someone laughed or made fun of you? Instead of your making progress, he stopped you. This other person impacted your reality.

Who we are in others' eyes affects our own reality as well as who we are in our own eyes. When someone looks at us in that wonderful way — makes eye contact and we know we're special — we rejoice in that.

The Winds of Change

Over time, it may also happen that a person who has valued us goes away. It hurts. Maybe we had a relationship with a special friend who would brighten up when they saw us, and vice versa. All of a sudden we see this person and expect that enthusiastic look and instead they've distanced themselves from us and become inattentive.

So we ask how they are, what's wrong? The person responds, "Nothing." But we already know something is different, because their eyes have told us so. Maybe there's been a change in the relationship that we've sensed. Maybe they are preoccupied with some personal issue that is troubling them. Eventually, we learn that something in fact has changed.

If we feel that the relationship is changing or that we are losing the relationship we had with them, we may be forced into the grieving process. The first thing we experience is denial — the first stage of grieving any loss as discussed in the previous chapter. We think, he says there is nothing wrong, so I probably made that up — I didn't see anything. The first thing we do may be to deny what we saw. We may even try to talk ourselves out of what we saw. But we saw it; the eyes reported it. Things have changed.

In the holding chapter, we learned that if we are not held we might not survive. While we don't need to be validated by someone else in order to survive and we are not going to die from lack of validation, it does give us encouragement and confidence to go on with our lives. Remember how wonderful it was to receive positive validation and how hurtful it was not to receive it? Therefore, we know that receiving or not receiving validation can change the quality of our life. When the quality of *life* changes, we find that the quality of *self* changes too.

ACTION ITEM··········►

Mapping Your Relationships

Refer back to your relationship maps and write a V for validation in the circle of those who are or have been nutritious and validating for you. Maybe this is a good time to call or email them to say thank you.

Validating Others and Ourselves
Bulletin Board

At first I thought, how dumb can you be to keep going back to someone who doesn't validate you? but then I realized I have been doing it most of my life. (Binny, 57)

If I ever catch myself being a gravel friend or associating with gravel people, I'll have to stop myself and go get some birdseed. (Nancy, 25)

I never realized just how many gravel friends I had. So many times I've tried to understand why I feel so drained when I am with some of these friends, but now I know. (Deborah, 27)

"Who we are in others' eyes affects our sense of our own reality." This statement made me take a deeper look into who's in my life and whom I'm allowing to create my reality. I didn't like the thought of giving someone else that much power. I am trying to take the gravel people out of my life. It seems like you have to recycle this process every few years. (Tamira, 33)

It's a wonderful and necessary feeling to feel we matter. (Jenna, 20)

As a little boy I was viewed more as a problem child who was to be contained rather than valued. (Isaac, 47)

Being known as I am without wearing masks to hide toxic shame is my road to healing. Amazing what a relief it is to be accepted as we are without having to be perfect. To be seen as who we are is liberating and I won't settle for masks or lies anymore. (Mary Lou, 46)

I remember the smiling eyes of total strangers in California. I think one of the American culture traits "smiling at strangers" is wonderful in terms of eye-to-eye validation. Those smiles from strangers may be just for a moment, but they at least tell me that I'm here. I've never received those smiles in Japan. (Jin, 20)

I am one of those people who ignore all the people who do validate me and specifically devote my energy to the one person who doesn't and can't (my dad). Because he himself has never been validated he has never learned how to validate others. I am now trying not to look to him for validation and to find it somewhere else. (Dawn, 19)

When I look at my little boys and they look back, I know and feel overwhelming love. They are my children and I will love them before I love myself. They need me, and I will provide for them and protect them. When they are sad, they look to me for comfort and validation of their feelings. (Jerry, 38)

When I went through a counseling process, the most important thing my therapist did for me was to validate me. I believe it was one of the keys to healing my life. (Wendellyn, 20)

I find myself on a constant search for validation: more is better. I strive to hear the words, "good job" or "I'm proud of you". (Paco, 20)

> To feel like someone understands me is very nurturing. (Katy, 38)

I read and walked for miles at night
along the beach,
Writing bad verse and searching
endlessly for
Someone wonderful who would step out
of the darkness
And change my life.
It never crossed my
mind that the
Person could be me.

—Anna Quindlen

Chapter 9

Mirrors with Agendas

While we assume that most mirrors reflect accurately, when the mirror is another person, we have to take into consideration their bias or agenda. What they choose to mirror or support may have more to do with them than the one who is being mirrored. How does it impact us if they only mirror their agenda? The concept we are looking at in this chapter is other people as mirrors for ourselves.

O
nce upon a time, a queen had a little daughter, who was as white as snow, and as red as blood, and her hair was as black as ebony, and she was called little Snow White. And when the child was born, the queen died.

After a year had passed the king took to himself another wife. She was a beautiful woman, but proud and haughty, and she could not bear that anyone else should surpass her in beauty. She had a wonderful looking-glass, and when she stood in front of it and looked at herself in it, she said,

"Looking-glass, looking-glass, on the wall,
Who in this land is the fairest of all?"

The looking-glass answered,

"Thou, o queen, art the fairest of all."

Then she was satisfied, for she knew that the looking-glass spoke the truth.

But Snow White was growing up, and grew more and more beautiful, and when she was seven years old she was as beautiful as the day, and more beautiful than the queen herself. And once when the queen asked her looking-glass,

"Looking-glass, looking-glass, on the wall, who in this land is the fairest of all?"

It answered,

"Thou art fairer than all who are here, lady queen. But more beautiful still is Snow White, as I ween."

Then the queen was shocked, and turned yellow and green with envy. From that hour, whenever she looked at Snow White, her heart heaved in her breast, she hated the girl so much. And envy and pride grew higher and higher in her heart like a weed, so that she had no peace day or night.

And you know the rest of the story. The evil queen's mirror is perhaps the most famous mirror of all.

A mirror is designed to reflect an image. We use mirrors for feedback and information. Sometimes we visit a mirror quickly as we check our reflection one more time for completeness on our way out the door. Other times, we gaze for a long time, evaluating, judging and seeking more information than we think we have. Do I look okay for this event? Do I look like I'm aging? What do people see in me today? Have I lost or gained weight? Is this color good for me? Will he think I'm attractive?

We use mirrors to reflect our image. Sometimes it's accurate and sometimes we see only what we want to see, not necessarily what is there. We might even be judgmental about our own reflections, especially on a bad hair day!

We use other people as mirrors for ourselves too. We ask, "What do you see when you look at me?" or "Do you think that I can do this or become this?"

Besides reflecting, what else do we know about mirrors? We may think they don't lie, but sometimes a mirror does lie. A fun house mirror lies on purpose; it is warped and distorted. When we talk about a mirror image, we have to consider whether the mirror has its own agenda.

There are bright and decorative mirrors. Lighting effects can impact what we see. Department stores are notorious for putting in "skinny" mirrors because they want to encourage us to buy. The lighting in the dressing room for women is usually soft so that they'll look better than usual. The more expensive the store, the more the mirrors and lighting are designed to enhance our image.

In our own mirrors, many times we do see ourselves differently. We may see beyond our own image to an imagined image of ourselves, maybe better than reality, maybe worse. It can vary depending on the day, or the hour. People reflect back to us an image. Sometimes the mirror image from the person is accurate; sometimes the mirror/person has his own agenda. From infancy, the reflections we get from others provide a form of reality.

Look at the different stages of our lives; each person who mirrors us does so in a unique way. Each relationship has its own mirror. Parents, family and caregivers mirror the infant. During our childhood schooling, each time we have a different teacher, we have a different mirror. Each time we have a different friend, we have a different mirror. When we go to college or take a job, each professor and each boss mirrors us again.

The feedback we receive is different with each mirror.

Every relationship reflects something to us. At each stage in our lives the self is once again reflected, reframed and sometimes reshaped based on the mirror the person holds up. There are people mirrors who insist on controlling another person and who reflect hurtful things in order to keep the person under their thumb. There are those who lovingly nurture. There are those who are demanding and challenging.

Take this example: If you went out for an athletic team and the coach said to you, "Well, you're probably a so-so performer, I don't expect much from you today," that's about what he would get from you. If the coach said to you, "You can do it, you can run faster, jump higher, score more; you're the best on the team—I'm counting on you," the mirror being held up says you can do it. That mirror is encouraging. We can have mirrors that encourage us or ones that discourage. Whatever the mirrors say frames and shapes our self. We notice the feedback and it can impact us.

With lots of positive feedback, the self grows and gets stronger. Negative feedback can either roll off our backs or slow us down. If the negative mirroring comes from an intimate relationship, the self can crumble because of the reflection it sees and receives. Even self-assured people can have their confidence eroded in a setting, which repeatedly puts them down or negates their contributions particularly if they do not have a positive support system away from that setting. The impact of being excluded or of getting condescending or dirty looks from our peers can be debilitating. A preteen or teenager can "look through" a peer with piercing precision causing chills and doubts in the receiver.

One of the saddest examples I can recount was that of a father putting down his eight-year-old son. He yelled at him, "You are not worth a pimple on a dead Marine's ass." The father said it to his son once. The emotional impact of the comment stayed with the son and he repeated it in his head for the next thirty-two years and wondered why he felt worthless.

In a supportive environment, he began to believe in himself more and to replace that toxic and stupid comment from his past with more positive messages. Obviously the father had received that comment in his military experience. I say it is a stupid comment because it was inappropriate, totally over the top and never anything to say to a developing young man.

As children we often have a lot of dreams that with support can become a reality. If there is lack of mirroring in the family, those dreams may become bruised, tempting us to hide them, or discard them outright.

Kathryn always wanted to be a rock star, but her family says, "You? You can't be a rock star; you don't know how to play an instrument. There's no way you'll ever be a rock star." At this point, Kathryn has a choice to believe them or to believe in her dream. If her family and friends don't mirror her dream, it might split off. Splitting off means she takes that little part of herself and distances herself from it and tries to starve it to death because it is too painful to hold on to. Although it was terribly important to her, it hurts too much to keep it alive. She gives up her dream.

Maybe your dream is to go to college, and your family says, "No one in our family goes to college, and you're much too stupid to do that." You get all this negative feedback and finally say, "I guess they're right." You then stop trying and when you stop trying, your dream splits off. As it splits off, you have a choice: You can either keep that part of yourself private and find a way to keep the dream alive or you can make it go away forever.

What is split off is sometimes a part of our selfhood—a part we give up because of the reaction of the people we have turned to for the mirroring.

As you think about it, what would be some of the things a

family might not mirror? It might be a certain talent that they don't like or understand or approve of. Confidence? Sometimes families or friends promote confidence and sometimes they take it away because they figure if they put you down, they'll be raised up.

We second-guess ourselves when people tell us we don't know what we're talking about. Has anyone ever said to you, "You are so clumsy?" And suddenly, you can't walk without stumbling. It becomes a matter of ear-to-ear lack of validation! Or in sports, our opponents try to psych us out with a comment that plants doubts in our skills and causes us to make an error.

What are some other things a family or friends may not validate?

- Someone who is smarter or less smart than the family norm or peer group may choose to hide her intelligence for fear of ridicule.
- If appearance — choice of dress, hairstyle, weight — falls out of the family's self-image or the peer group's "uniform", there may be discomfort.
- Someone may judge another's success. A family may not like another's success if they didn't have the same type of success or status. This could relate to finances or achievements. It can be a sports family with a family member who wants to be a computer programmer or an astrophysicist.
- It can be a musical family with someone who rejects music in favor of following a trade.

If you approach your parents and say, "Hi, Mom and Dad, I'm gay." Their first response may be, "No you're not." If you have come to the realization that you're a gay person and you tell your family and they reject that, you have choices. You can accept that others have problems understanding differences, you can keep it secret or you can try to change what you believe about yourself and make it go away. In that case, the self splits off.

Trying to make your *self* go away is a very painful process. Because of that, the suicide rate in young gay teenagers is extremely high. Many times they lack support for a choice, or a biological fact that they are trying to deal with. Some gay teens are asked by their families to leave. Then they must search out new families and friends to feel a sense of belonging again.

There are many categories of differences where a family might not mirror who you are becoming, or a behavior you are trying on (i.e., a different religion, political differences, an interracial relationship, a different career). Sometimes, we just have to give our families time to get used to new ideas.

I counseled a young pregnant couple, both sixteen years old, who wanted to have their baby. Their families had a very difficult time with this. The young people said they wanted to have a family, except they wanted their parents to take care of the baby and its expenses. The parents objected, saying, "We are having a little trouble mirroring this; this is not what we want for you and not what we want for our lives right now." And they have a right to their own lives too.

The teens didn't want to be parents; they didn't plan on it. But there is a baby coming. The timing and circumstances did not allow for any other option, regardless of their beliefs. Maybe you or someone you know had children at an early age. The decision for this young couple is what to do; do we keep our baby or give it up for adoption? All four parents of the teens are saying that they should put the child up for adoption. The teens are saying they want to keep the baby.

One set of information is: let's be realistic, you're too young, etc. There are many reasons it would be better to put the child up for adoption. Then there are the feelings of the teen parents-to-be who want to keep the baby. The realistic side of it is what do we do? The grandparents-to-be don't want to raise another baby, and the children who are having the baby are saying if their parents will take care of the baby for a couple of years, then they will be old enough to take care of the baby later. They want to keep the baby!

Here are the competing agendas: The grandparents-to-be have an agenda; the mother-to-be has an agenda, the father-to-be has a different agenda, and the baby has an agenda. How do you take all those agendas and sort out a workable solution? Well, first of all, the grandparents-to-be are still dealing with the advice they gave to the teens: we told you not to have sex, why did you have sex? How long have you been having sex? Why didn't you use protection?

The conflict in families is that young people want to be mirrored or supported for decisions they are making, which the elders many times don't approve of and which directly affect the elder's lives too. That's conflict. There are differences of opinion, different lifestyles or different experiences, which may cause them to mirror or not mirror certain behaviors. There are also actions and consequences.

It's sad when we have something we really want to do, or something we really want to try on, and we can't find a mirror for it in our immediate family. What we have to do is go outside the family and find another mirror. Maybe your immediate family isn't going to mirror what you're doing or the behavior you're trying on right now. You may need to find someone else who does support and mirror you. Another option is to reevaluate your choices in light of the family values. Is what you are doing hurtful to you?

If I hold up a mirror and you don't like it—you have a choice. You don't have to accept the perceptions or mirroring of another. One of the things I would encourage you to do is to look behind the mirror. What kind of a mirror is this? What is the agenda of this mirror? What kind of feedback are you looking for? Are you looking for permission? Is this mirror warning you of danger? Is this mirror a positive support for you or is this someone only concerned with their own best interests?

The wicked queen in Snow White asked her mirror a question while fishing for a compliment and then got angry at the truth that the mirror delivered.

If your parent says to you, "I'm concerned about you being involved with someone of a different religion," what kinds of things might be behind a statement like that? The mirroring concept is all about feedback. It's oftentimes a reflection of the opinions of the person you have asked for feedback. Much of your dependence on this mirroring depends on how you feel about the person you have invited to mirror you.

Some people choose mirrors that have their best interests at heart while others choose those that can do them harm. "I'm going to find the most unforgiving and critical mirror I can, and that's what I'm going to pay attention to." Or, "I'm going to find the most flattering mirror, and that's what I'm going to pay attention to." We do have choices about some of our mirrors. Others come with the family. It's only when we have the sense that we have only one mirror — it's only what the family says, it's only what my mate says, or what my best friend says — that we limit the feedback.

It's important to know that no matter how together you are, even the most together person — taken out of an environment which is supportive — may go to pieces. Perhaps you go into a situation saying you're strong and ready for everything, but if your support systems dissolve, that confidence may leave. A strong family or a good relationship can give the support to succeed in difficult environments. The absence of that support will allow a toxic person to have an impact on you that can erode and damage your performance and your sense of self. In the absence of something or someone supporting you, you can lose that center of yourself no matter how together you are.

What we find is that the un-mirrored self can break into pieces. "I can't find anyone to support me in this—I'm in a job where no one is supporting me—or I'm living in a community where no one is supporting me and I'm fragmenting—I'm going to pieces."

My advice for someone who is in a job where no one is supporting the work they are doing, is that there are other jobs—you don't have to stay there and watch yourself erode. You can change your attitude or change your job. While this is sometimes easier said than done, the timing for leaving can be of your choosing. An exit strategy makes the time that you choose to remain more manageable. All of the above applies to relationships as well.

If you're in a relationship where it seems you're only being criticized—nothing is written in stone that says you have to stay there. It doesn't mean don't *work* at a relationship, it means don't *stay* in one that has nothing for you.

Remember that the self grows in the presence of interpersonal nutrients. So when I'm in a nutritious situation, my self is growing. If the nutrients are gone and all I have around me is gravel, or all that is mirrored is rejection, I fragment. I go to pieces. I cut away those parts of my self that are deemed unacceptable.

Sometimes we don't want to take any chances, so we don't let anyone know about our dreams. We don't trust anyone with them. We wish to preserve the self by keeping it hidden. By keeping it hidden, we protect ourselves but we don't become who we authentically are. We miss some joy in our lives.

In relationships, mirroring and reflecting takes place. It's not just about someone agreeing with us all the time. Sometimes the best feedback is from someone who is willing to disagree with us in a constructive way. That's the way we grow. Sometimes the positive support can come from work, school or perhaps a group of friends you surround yourself with. One positive person with honest feedback can be a powerful ally.

On the other hand, one toxic person can obliterate a completely good environment. Sometimes the reason we stay in unhealthy relationships is because of a money issue, a control issue or because we have lost our sense of self.

Sooner or later we reach a point where either we must change, or we need to change our circumstances. We want to be understood, to be known, to be accepted by someone, or a few some ones—people who say, "I know who you are, and that's fine with me." This is a step towards creating togetherness that works.

I saw an old movie recently, where two people were getting married and took a minister down to the beach with them to perform the ceremony. Their marriage vows were, "We take each other *as is*." *As is* is an acceptance—whoever you are, whatever you are, I accept you *as is*. And, perhaps as whom you are becoming. That is nutritious.

ACTION ITEM ·········►

Mapping Your Relationships

Review your relationship maps and mark the circles of those who have mirrored you in a positive way with an MP (mirrored positively).

If you have toxic people in your life, write in your journal about how you would feel if you could separate yourself from them.

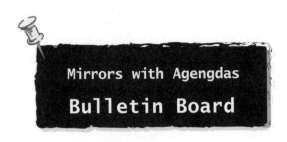

I was real to Mary so I felt some realness to myself. Mary always looked at me with eyes that believed I could do and be anything I wanted to be. She mirrored me in a very positive and pleasurable way. She looked at me like I mattered, like my dreams mattered. She wanted for me what I wanted for myself. I was special to Mary. I meant something to her. (Marlise, 25)

> My mother loved to show me off. It was her way of showing off what a perfectly cute little baby she'd had. I wish it had been more about me than just about how cool she was. (Celia, 29)

My supervisor for the past ten years, who did not support me as a person—but who did value my work—has transferred to a different department. I now report to a different person who supports me as a person as well as my work. It is a real morale booster. We have a really good working relationship that we both enjoy and actually have fun with. I always thought that it didn't bother me that my old supervisor didn't respect me as a person. I was just kidding myself. Sometimes you don't realize how bad something is until you realize how good it can be. (Diana, 34)

> It truly seems to be that my not letting anyone mirror me is the main reason I do not feel mirrored. (Kendra, 20)

I hope to raise positive, happy, sensitive and respectful children. I want my children never to be afraid to talk to me about things that may be bothering them. When I was younger I had low self-esteem and I wasn't happy with myself. I want my children to take pride in themselves because it sure feels wonderful. I believe that every single one of us has a special significance. (Verda, 32)

I used to have a strong sense of who I was, but over the years my self got blurred with all the things that others told me I was. I have decided that, when in doubt, I will think back to who I was when I was ten. That is closer to my true self than what the people in my life have come to see me as now. I now concentrate on being who I really am and won't compromise. (Nica, 21)

I oftentimes feel that I act very outgoing and at times slightly obnoxious in order to divert people from looking at the real me. That way I know if they make fun of me or don't like me, then I can say, well that's not really me, that's only who I pretend to be. (Susy, 22)

I remember my parents saying, "That B on your report card could have been an A." I never felt 'good enough'. (Karen, 25)

Presently I am trying to find out who I really am. I have let so many people change my identity in order to be accepted that I have lost that sense of where my identity ends and where the other person in my life begins. It's as if I've taken on so many different personas that I don't know which one I am. (Winter, 26)

The only time my father looked at me was when he was angry or when he was torturing me with constant teasing. I remember how much my father's eyes scared me. I did not want him to look at me. I did not want anyone to look at me. I just wanted to be left alone. (Alma, 43)

Oh, come on, Bev, there might be some
great guys here tonight!

Chapter 10

Relating Sexually

"If sex is such a natural phenomenon, how come there are so many books on how to do it?"
— Bette Midler

The hormonal cocktail impacts us even when we say we are in control. In particular, this chapter discusses the love hormone oxytocin and how it leads us around by the nose—or are those the pheromones talking?

As we approach this chapter on relating sexually, I wonder what I can add that you haven't already heard before. How can I present old and new material so that you will get some different information, at least in a fresh way, to draw on as you make very personal decisions that are extremely important to your life?

Let's start with what you already know . . .

What did your parents tell you about sex? Perhaps some of these answers fit for you.

- Nothing.
- Everything.
- Don't do it.
- It's bad.
- Wait until you are older.
- You need to be responsible and mature.
- It's sacred.
- Be safe.
- Get married first.

- Be careful.
- Nice girls don't do it!
- Get what you can without getting caught (father to son).

You got all these messages...and then you got a few more!

- Men will lie and say anything in order to have sex.
- The girl is trying to trap you.
- Don't do it because they're lying about loving you.
- Girls have sex in order to get love.
- Guys pretend to love in order to get sex.

Did these messages matter to you? In what way? How old were you when you started getting these messages? High school? Junior high? Elementary school? When you were old enough to ask questions about it? Perhaps you had sex education as a class in school.

Parents face a dilemma. What do they tell their kids and when should they talk to them about sex and sexuality? This can be a difficult conversation to have. Yet, media exposure today forces parents into this discussion earlier than they might wish in order to answer children's questions. And kids seem understandably reluctant to share this part of their lives openly with parents in expectation of their disapproval.

A little boy came home from school and asked his mom where he came from. So his mother figured the timing was right and she went over all the reproductive biological information with him. When she finished, she asked if he had any questions. He then said, "Well, Mom, that's very interesting, but Billie is from Pittsburgh and I want to know where I came from."

We have been given a lot of advice, but how many of us actually followed it? Precious few! And it was such good advice! Isn't that interesting?

Where do we get information about sex?

- Friends
- Internet
- TV
- Movies
- Books
- Magazines
- Parents (if we are lucky)

How do we determine which information is meaningful and helpful versus useless or inaccurate nonsense?

As we try to make sense of our own sexuality, we listen to other people's experiences. We hear about sex at church, from religious groups, friends, adults, movies, in books, and we are left with confusion. Again, which info is helpful and which is useless? **In fact, when it comes to sex we behave as if we don't believe any of the information or advice that we have been given.**

A third grader had a lesson about AIDS in school. When he returned home, his mother asked, "What did you learn today?" He said, "Well, we learned how to avoid intersections and how to use condominiums." That's the kind of sense it made to him.

Sex is a popular subject with comedians. Zsa Zsa Gabor quipped, "Personally I know nothing about sex because I have always been married." And Lily Tomlin stated, "Sexual freedom means freedom from having sex."

Then we have wonderful experts on sex like the characters in the movie *When Harry Met Sally*. Have you seen it? If you haven't, rent it and be prepared for a lot of laughs; you'll see relationships in a different way. In that film, Harry says, "You have sex and the minute you finish, you know what goes through your mind? How long do I have to hold her before I can get up and go home? Is thirty seconds enough?" What this is, is sex. But it's not a sexual relationship. It has nothing to do with the needs of both people building togetherness.

What is passionate experience? How do we learn about it? What models do we have?

When early TV shows were about to show a sex scene, the screen would fade to black. The couple looked at each other longingly and then the image dissolved or cut to another scene of action. We thought we knew what the couple was going to do, but we never actually saw it. We wondered but could only imagine what they were doing. And, they all had separate beds. Episodes of "I Love Lucy" showed her and Ricky, a young married couple, in twin beds. Imagine!

Do you think that everything we see in the movies is real? We expect that if we see a good movie that it's going to have sex scenes in it. Even prime time TV programs regularly include a few sexy moments. (We expect it to have some plot to it also.) For some people, the only sex education they receive is from the movies they see.

Today, there is explicit information about sex that is available to any person of any age or level of maturity whether or not they want it. I read that a senator's daughter typed in her name on the Internet and up came a porn site. She's a little kid. She has more information than she can possibly deal with. It is many times less than accurate information too.

It is information—but it is not applied knowledge. You might ask what the difference is. In our lives we are inundated with tons of information. Much of it is questionable and unless we take the time to verify it, we may find it to be misleading. When we do verify it, then we need to decide what to do with it and to see if it can be applied to our lives. Some information can be wrong or hurtful. Sifting through the information and deciding if it is right for us is the process of building knowledge.

ACTION ITEM ··········➤

Count the "Fs" Test

Count the Fs in the following sentence and write the number of Fs that you see in the little box.

FINISHED FILES ARE THE RESULT
OF YEARS OF SCIENTIFIC STUDY
COMBINED WITH THE EXPERIENCE
OF MANY YEARS.

How many Fs did you see?

Three? Four? Five? Six? Three is a right answer; there are three Fs. Five is a right answer—there are five Fs, and six is the right answer, as there are six Fs in the sentence.

So how can that be? You look at this sentence and you see three Fs and wonder how anyone can see six Fs—that can't be right. If you saw six Fs, you are wondering, "what is so hard about seeing all six of them?" I wonder if you saw five, why you didn't see six. One person I know saw four at first and then could only see three—how come?

The right answer is six. Most people tend to see three. All the Fs are right in front of your eyes. Perhaps you still don't see all of them—so what are you ignoring? Little words! It seems like they are hidden from you. If you still only see three, look at the three times *of* appears in the sentence.

Surprised? Instead of saying *of*, we hear *ov*. If you show this to a half a dozen people, one of them might see six, but most of them will see three.

Here's the purpose of the test . . .

It is about what we choose to pay attention to and what we choose to ignore. You were making a decision as you looked at this. You made a decision as to what you would pay attention to and what you would ignore.

145

Relating Sexually

It isn't that you don't want to see them. It's that you've made a conscious or unconscious decision about what you're going to pay attention to and what you're going to ignore. We're trained to skip the little things and concentrate on the big things.

We do this in life. I'm going to choose to pay attention to this, and not pay attention to that. And when we come to the area of sex, believe me, we choose what we're going to pay attention to and what we're going to ignore. And all that advice we heard? Did we pay attention to it or ignore it?

We have gender differences, as well, which means we pay attention differently. The masculine self is defined by *doing*; the feminine by *being*. Men *do*, women *be*. For men, sexuality is more focused in the genitals—it is external. For women it is more likely located in the heart—it's internal. We're built differently. Men have an external sexuality and women have an internal sexuality. Differences tend to lead to behavioral differences too. Men are overt and open in their sexuality while women tend to behave covertly sexually. Thus, we have major differences and confusion at times.

So, how many Fs do you see? As we go through this chapter, take notice of what you choose to pay attention to and what you choose to ignore.

Remember the sixteen-year-old girl and sixteen-year-old boy who are soon to be parents from Chapter 9? In addition to all the other circumstances, they are all back dealing with the issue we are talking about right now, which is, what do you pay attention to and what do you ignore? The grandparents-to-be are still dealing with the advice they gave to the teens: we told you not to have sex, why did you have sex? How long have you been having sex? Why didn't you use protection? If you had all that information and we told you not to get pregnant, how did this happen? My answer is, "the usual way!"

The teenagers never meant to get pregnant. Sex was an adventure between them. Hormones were a driving force. It felt like they were in love. It feels good, and it's fun and any other assortment of reasons.

What we choose to pay attention to and what we choose to ignore can be impacted by our upbringing, our attention span and even our hormones. Hormones insist that we pay attention to them.

The Hormonal Cocktail

There are hormonal reasons for bonding. Humans have a potent "hormonal cocktail" that causes even powerful people to act foolishly. We've seen examples of that in our country. Hormones drive an entire entertainment industry and they regularly distract young people from life goals. We react sexually but have not developed a mature respect for the *power* of it.

Sex itself is simple; animals do it. Sexuality is normal and natural. Sexual feelings are normal and natural. BUT, sexual relationships are complex and difficult. They are difficult because they involve communication and the other needs we have in connecting to another human being. **Having sex is different from having a sexual relationship.**

The hormonal cocktail is made up of a number of different things:

- Testosterone — the male sex hormone
- Estrogen — the female sex hormone
- Pheromones — scent
- Oxytocin — the bonding hormone

Men have estrogen to go with their testosterone and women have testosterone to go with their estrogen. One of the things I think is curious is the switch in hormone power as we age. A young male has an increase in puberty of twenty to forty times his previous level of testosterone, and a young female entering puberty has a three-fold increase of estrogen. Later in life, as the male and female age, the woman's level of estrogen drops and her level of testosterone gets higher. When the male is aging, his level of testosterone declines, while his level of estrogen rises.

Stereotypically, the male was perhaps interested in going out and conquering the business world, and was more assertive and aggressive in his approach to business, money making, running the family, sex, organizing and being in charge of male type things. As he ages, he becomes far more interested in staying home. We find Grandma and Grandpa changing roles. Grandma says she wants to get active in politics now that the kids are gone. "I want to be part of a political action group, and get a job." Meanwhile, Grandpa is saying, "Can't we just hang around the home and *be*?"

The switch in roles seems to correlate with the switch in these two hormones.

I invite you to visit my web site at **www. janfritsen.com** for more on what I'm about to share with you. The Resources section of the web site provides links to articles on oxytocin.

The information is new enough that we are making some guesses about what it means, and how it applies to our growing understanding about our sexual relationships. It seems to make sense. Perhaps you have already seen something about this on TV or in a magazine article. I think you'll be hearing more about it.

Let's take a fresh look at what we know about oxytocin.

What we have known ...

We have known about some uses of oxytocin for a long time. We know oxytocin stimulates labor. The pituitary gland of a woman about to go into labor releases oxytocin in order to promote uterine contractions and to help deliver the baby.

I had a paramedic in a class who said he carried oxytocin in his kit. With a woman who is having trouble delivering, they give her an injection of oxytocin.

The second thing we know is that oxytocin helps the

mother to bond with her baby. While she is nursing, more oxytocin is released, which gives her warm, connected feelings to the baby. The bonding of a mother with her child happens in part because of the hormone oxytocin.

So what is new?

This may be news to you. I credit Dr. Pat Allen, a well-known author, therapist and speaker on relationships for introducing me to this information and for some of the language of this discussion.

Let me start by asking you a question...

Do you know someone, particularly a young woman, who has been in a relationship and is trying to get out of it? You hear her say things like, "He's a total jerk and I'll never have anything to do with him again." The next thing you know, they are back together. Do you know someone like that? Unfortunately, it appears this is common.

Part of the *why* of this has to do with oxytocin. So please pay attention.

Oxytocin is activated during sexual stimulation, and it is reactivated any time the five senses are engaged (hearing, seeing, smelling, tasting, touch). You touch, smell, taste, see him, or you hear him after being sexually stimulated and it's like you get a fresh "dose" of oxytocin. Oxytocin is designed to help us bond. Dr. Allen would say that women not only bond, they glue! This then is more than a casual connection.

Oxytocin is an addictive neurotransmitter that is a lot like an amphetamine. Its make-up includes a compound that is found in chocolate. Chocolate is a first cousin to having sex. Imagine.

For this discussion, set aside what you already know about the cultural side of sex and the habits of the day. The purpose of oxytocin is this: the female and the male get together sexually, have very good feelings and they procreate—they have babies. The biological purpose of a male and female union is not only for sexual release but also to have a family and to stay bonded.

The function of oxytocin is to keep the female bonded, monogamous and to continually encourage the good feelings of the relationship that were there at the beginning. In other words, it's the refresher, the hormone that keeps the sexual relationship alive. The attraction doesn't get old and stale because it's continually re-stimulated. This contributes to keeping a couple together. Women bond with their babies and they bond with the person who stimulates them sexually.

By the end of this lecture, the women in class wanted to borrow some oxytocin and inject their boyfriends with it!

Advice to Wise Men!

A wise man wishing to keep his woman happy touches her, kisses her and lets her wear his shirt, so that when he's absent she still has his scent. His scent is also known as a pheromone —a scent that both men and women give off.

Giving your shirt to your girlfriend when she is sick, or so she can sleep in it: 1) Gives off your scent, 2) releases oxytocin, and 3) contributes to the bonding.

Oxytocin is released when any of the five senses are stimulated. What that does is to re-stimulate the feelings of the first sexual arousal from your partner. You bond, you glue, and it is designed to keep you interested in your partner.

Because the neurotransmitter is activated, one of the things that happens is that you lose the capacity of discernment in the brain—you go temporarily nuts—you can't and aren't thinking—you are feeling. You are addicted to the good feelings of oxytocin. When you are feeling, you are not thinking. Thinking is a step removed.

If away on a trip what might a wise male do to keep his presence active in his woman's mind? Remembering that these things activate oxytocin, he might call her, text message, send a picture or chocolate, send flowers and send a slightly sweaty shirt!

Let's switch things around. Despite what parents want to believe, many young people are experimenting with sex at a frighteningly early age. The meaning of it all for some young people has been reduced to just something to do. They're trying to have casual sex, which they refer to as friendship with benefits. So a teenager might think, "Well, everyone is doing it—I may as well try it." I hear a lot of young women say they are very eager to get rid of their virginity—as if it's a burden. After her first sexual experience, one young woman said, "I finally feel like I accomplished something." In her mind, this stood out ahead of all the other things in her life that she had learned and experienced. She wanted to feel special and to be valued. She wanted to experience sex.

So, young people have a casual sexual experience, and then they say, "Wow, what are these feelings?" What has been activated is all of the bonding mechanisms, and now the thinking is, "Wait a minute, this was supposed to be casual—I didn't mean for it to be serious—and now I want to bond with him. This must be love because of the feelings I have."

She is no longer feeling casual about this experience. Right here is the magic of, and the problem with oxytocin. This is why Dr. Allen says, "Women, do not have casual sex unless you are man enough to do it!" There is no such thing as casual sex for you if oxytocin becomes activated and you bond with this person you are trying to treat casually. You can't do it.

With an emotional, sexual bond comes the release of oxytocin. If you break up, part of your pain will come from a chemical withdrawal. If you have been sexually, chemically connected and you've done some thinking which has caused you to leave the relationship, you still have to get over the chemical connection with that person. You're going to miss him. That process of detox takes up to two years. Yes, up to two years!

The younger the person, the more likely they are to say, "We're breaking up, but we're still going to be friends. And I can kiss him sometimes because we're friends. And, because we were such good friends, sometimes we can still have sex."

And that is why they can't move on, and get past this relationship. Confused? Go back and reread about oxytocin!

Pheromones

Pheromones relate to the scent we give off and whether or not we're attracted to someone. It doesn't have to do with whether or not a person is clean; it's a scent issue. There are people who smell good to us, and those who don't. We respond to our friends because they smell good to us. We don't usually walk up to our friends and sniff them to see how they smell. We are talking about a subtle scent that is given off by the person.

You can buy pheromones in department stores, and purchasers attest to the fact that when they wear it, other people are attracted to them. You can purchase "Falling in Love" by the ounce. Philosophy cosmetics makes the product and claims "the concoction is laced with pheromones — those odorless, airborne molecules, synthesized from human chemical secretions that are purported to boost attractiveness."

A recent experiment used an estrogen-like chemical distilled from women's urine and a testosterone chemical from male sweat. Using MRI and PET scans the researchers found that when women sniffed male pheromones, their hypothalamuses lit up and in men the results were the opposite. While this is not too surprising, when gay males were exposed to male pheromones, their hypothalamuses lit up while female pheromones did nothing for them. Interesting?

A professor of anatomy and neuro-biology at U.C. Irvine forecasts that, "In ten years or less there could be brain chemical nasal sprays to enhance love between partners." Just "sniff" and the other person looks pretty good!

Inevitable Changes

What we want when we are in a relationship at age sixteen is very different from what we want when we're twenty-six, thirty-six and fifty-six. If the relationship choice changes, you have some decisions to make because no relationship stands still—EVER.

Both of you are going to grow and change. If you do it in a compatible way, it becomes the staying power for you to remain together in the future. If one person changes and the other doesn't, that which worked in the beginning won't continue to work.

Here's a rule—we always modify each other in relationships. When we are in a relationship, you change me and I change you. We modify each other because when we're together, whoever you are rubs off on me and whoever I am rubs off on you. Pretty soon we pick up each other's words, phrases, mannerisms and habits. People can tell we've been hanging out together because maybe we finish the other person's sentences and we know what they are going to think before they say it.

Sometimes we're right—sometimes we're really wrong. We get into habits that have to do with having *modified* each other.

The Arousal Template

Our first experience with sexual arousal is so powerful that it can become a template or pattern for arousal in the future —even into adulthood. This template incorporates life experiences that are connected to our sexual experiences. It becomes a sexual belief system or personal sexual map. Each of us carries in the cerebral cortex of the brain what psychologists call a love map.

Protecting children from too early exposure to sexual activity can help them to develop healthy attitudes and reactions to relating sexually. Protecting children can help them to develop a healthy love map to follow into adulthood.

When we meet someone who may be a potential partner, we make a judgment as to their being sexually attractive to us. Subconsciously, we evaluate or measure everyone we meet against this template or criteria that we have developed from that first arousal experience.

The Positive Relationship

When you really fall for someone and you're in a relationship where you're growing in your sexual communication and reducing boundaries (which happens over time), you are also growing in other ways. You're growing together in terms of your goals and your appreciation of the other person's qualities, other than sexual prowess, although that's good too. That growth is a mature change which begins to notice things beyond the superficial, such as "I really like how kind you are to others, how you are in business, that you are honest and giving, how you are being successful in whatever you do well, and in particular, how you _____ (you fill in the blank here with your custom compliment!).

Being a Priority!

No matter which gender we are, we want to be *special*. Many of us put monogamy and trust on our shopping lists. There are a lot of ways that we feel particular and special when it comes to love. We're particular and special as a mother, daughter, son, father, friend, aunt, uncle, cousin, neighbor—and we can love in those forms of relatedness. However, we can also have many friends and love them—many daughters, sons, aunts and uncles, and love them.

In the case of a passionate experience, each person wants to be special and particular. When we are the objects of someone else's sexual love and we know it is just for us and they know it's just for them, then there is a safety and a trust factor, which allows it to be special and to grow. This is one of the biggest arguments, in addition to oxytocin, against casual sex. We're not particular or special in casual sex. We wish to be chosen, and we wish to be a priority to someone else.

You know in your relationships what your priority ranking is. Sometimes you can be in a relationship and be about number six on their priority list. Their job, car, pet, ex-girlfriend, computer, and finally, number six is you! That doesn't feel good. What you really want is to be priority number one.

In a sexual relationship if you want to be safe, secure, satisfied and able to grow, it means being a priority and not being in competition. If you are in competition, "How did I do? How was I compared to number one or number two? are the questions that come to mind." It hurts to be compared to an ex-wife or ex-husband or other girlfriend or boyfriend. Ouch!

Again, the power of oxytocin, when we are sexually active, changes us. It changes the way we see the world. It modifies our behavior—it *and* the person we are with change our behavior. We change. When it's someone with whom we wish to share our lives, it's a wonderful experience. It can be a time of energy and renewal and joy.

The Rules

As humans, we have many openings in our bodies that are designed to take in information.

If you think about it, we have rules about all of these openings: what the eyes are supposed to see, what we're supposed to stick our nose in, rules about keeping our mouth shut, what we're supposed/not supposed to hear. And we certainly have rules about our genitals. We have rules about how we're supposed to behave sexually. Whether or not we behave that way depends on some other things, but we at least have rules about them.

Related to the rules, we have all sorts of guilt and frustration, and as a culture we're preoccupied with the whole subject. We have kinky talk shows on TV, showing people who are breaking all the rules in the most creative ways. These shows don't help with relationships; they are just supposed to be entertaining and shocking.

We have a great deal more information about what is wrong, rather than what is right about behavior and relationships.

HIV/AIDS

I can't leave this subject without once again commenting on safer sex.

We have this dilemma—sex is fun, being close to another person is what we want—it's normal and natural. While we used to fear becoming pregnant or getting a sexually transmitted disease, the danger of AIDS has changed our focus. We need to remember that AIDS is 100 percent preventable, as it is 100 percent fatal.

Therefore, I recommend that if you decide to be sexually active with someone, please get an HIV test. Make the agreement with your partner that if you're attracted enough to each other to have sex, that you not have sexual intercourse until you've both had a test. Wait for the results, share the results and then practice safer sex and monogamy.

Here's the rule: "No glove, no love." You can get tests done at Planned Parenthood, a county clinic, through the AIDS Response programs in your area or the county health agency in your area.

A message to parents of urgent importance: Your children need to hear out loud from you the words "I love you." They need your time and attention regularly. If they don't get that at home, they will seek it in the arms of someone ready to be sexual with them regardless of how young they are and regardless of the risks.

Advice just in case you daters are listening: For those of you that may be single and dating, "If you've been drinking, you're probably not thinking." If you make the decision to be sexually active, do it wisely because you're probably betting your life. DO NOT COUNT ON OTHER PEOPLE TO BE RESPONSIBLE FOR YOUR HEALTH!

When we talk about the sexual relationship, we're talking about something more than just having sex. We are including valuing and supporting, holding, and attaching to another person. Passion alone does not keep a couple together.

ACTION ITEM ·········▶

Questions for You to Ponder—Before Becoming Involved

▶ Who *are* you in a relationship?

▶ What qualities and skills do you have to bring to a relationship that you would consider perfect for you?

▶ What do you want in a loving relationship that you could and would commit to?

▶ Would the things you have listed bring you energy, the sense of being loved and the desire to stay in a committed relationship with this person?

▶ What are the rules about sex that you learned in your family? Do any of these rules need to be unlearned?

▶ What are the rules about sex that your partner learned in his/her family? How are they different from your rules?

▶ Do you have any fears about sex? Can you discuss them with your partner?

▶ What, if anything, did you learn in this chapter that has shifted your thinking?

Write about this in your journal.

Mapping Your Relationships

Review your relationship maps and mark with a SR those persons with whom you have had a sexual relationship, not just sex.

I lost my virginity to my best friend and this was okay because I figured we weren't going to hate each other later or have our friendship ruined. Unfortunately, I thought wrong. As it turned out, my feelings changed, maybe not because of the fact that he was "my first" but because I realized that we were perfect for each other and I wanted to be with him. He didn't feel the same, and as of today we are no longer friends. (Orlie, 20)

> We were both our firsts. Neither of us had experienced very much in the sexual department in prior relationships. We took everything very slow, and eventually we had sex. It was a period of experimentation that lasted at least six to seven months before we had sex. During that time period in which we both did everything for the first time together, I learned to like to do sexual acts through emotion first. I cannot stand doing anything sexual if I do not have feelings for someone. I believe that my sexual experience with her set me up with a nice template of sexual experience and allowed me to link emotion, affection and sexuality. (David, 19)

I don't really feel like I have ever made love with anyone; I feel like I've just had sex. (Marilyn, 20)

> Oxytocin! Oxytocin! Oxytocin! What can I say but crap. Why do we have to have this female bonding chemical? Why can't we be just like guys? Instead, we have this female bonding chemical that is like glue. That makes me attached to those creeps. Yes, I probably shouldn't have been around them in the first place but I was attached to them for some odd reason. Thank you so much for this wonderful news that it might be chemicals taking part in some of these messed up attachments and not my heart and my mind being stupid. It makes me think that I was not as stupid (when it comes to guys and me being attached to them) as I thought I was. (Dawn, 19)

All women ask themselves, since we love each other, shouldn't we make love? Wrong! My advice is, don't do it. Because you guys think you are thinking the same, but you're not. Men are thinking of arriving at passionate love through sex, while women find passionate sex through love. Talking about this in a group really helped me get through my pain. (Toni, 26)

> I really enjoyed learning about oxytocin. The whole topic of passionate experience was a real eye-opener for me. I found that oxytocin was a most intriguing thing. It made me think of how I felt at certain points in my past relationships with men. It's like the missing link! (Franky, 47)

I have made a vow to stay a virgin until I am married, and I have kept it. There isn't even a spiritual reason for it. I just want to show my husband how much I love him by saving it for him. I see it as the one real wedding gift from me that he will cherish. I want to be with someone who respects my decision and won't pressure me. By abstaining, I think it leaves room to get to know the person spiritually. Of course, I *do* want to be with a person that I am physically attracted to. (Sandy, 28)

> I discovered my sexuality in the beginning of high school. I had little if any self-esteem, but I had the need to be validated by someone. I felt very alone and unsure of myself. I met lots of guys who weren't very interested in me, just my body. They never held me, which was all I wanted. None of them ever listened or understood me. (Winter, 19)

My experiences of passion were to have sex. I always ended up feeling disgusted. My expectations of falling in love were what I saw in movies, always waiting for my prince to rescue me. I had horrible role models who did not express healthy ways of love, passion or even sex. This was not talked about or even physically expressed between my parents. As far as my mother was concerned, sex was only to be utilized if planning for a baby. (Sharon, 45)

> I got into a new relationship that had lots of intensity. For two years we fought and made love like crazy. Our sex life was great and proved that interpersonal conflict itself can be arousing. That

relationship was painful for me, but I couldn't leave it. We tried breaking up a lot and I remember thinking at one point, I'm dead, I'm walking around dead and nobody knows it. I suppose the fear of emotional deadness is what kept me in that relationship too long. (Tina, 40)

After we broke up, I ended up looking for that sense of security through another passionate experience, which only lasted one night. I realized that I had really made a mistake with that and that the sex was not what I was looking for. Now I look for someone that I can really get to know and trust and someone that I can share my own personal feelings with. I think I was looking for that all along, but I just couldn't put it into words. (Izzy, 26)

I've always considered myself a passionate and romantic man, and after we broke up I began dating other girls quite frequently. As this part of my life blossomed I realized that once I had sex with someone I would immediately notice his or her bad qualities and would leave. This pretty much led to just having sex. But recently over the past year I find myself searching for the "one". I have become more concerned with getting to know the person first rather than jumping into bed with her, something I did with my first love. And with this I feel I have made a full circle in the passionate experience category. (Jake, 24)

I had a very difficult time getting over my first love. It now makes sense why it was so hard. The emotional bond was also physiologically based. I know that oxytocin works with all five senses and I have resisted looking at any old photos. I know it will take two years to detox from the oxytocin. This is a long time and it will be difficult. Especially because I need to get my furniture out of his house at some point and it would be nice to be able to wait for two years, but that is not reasonable. In any case, I will limit contact as much as possible. (Tammy, 35)

I have always been the guy to cuddle before anything sexual and I think that it works great. I'm not saying that I did the holding to get the sex, but it seemed to work out that way. I never had a casual sexual relationship as I was with the same girl for five years, but it seemed to me that in that relationship the cuddling was the best part. We had a great sexual relationship, but I believe it was because we could cuddle and hold each other so nicely. (Aaron, 24)

I realized that I was substituting sex for being loved, and it was never satisfying. Holding is important, as long as both people understand each other. You can't have just a physical relationship. (Bonnie, 26)

I was the last one to have had sex out of all my friends. I met this guy who my friends thought was so cute. I was seventeen. He was everything I wanted in a guy, so I thought! He was cute and he had a nice car. I knew nothing about the inside of this so-called perfect guy. Finding out way too fast and finding myself stuck, I got pregnant very early into the relationship. That is what I mean by being stuck. The saddest part was not only was I stuck, I was stupid. I was allowing this guy to rule everything. I was nothing in his eyes. And slowly but surely I became nothing in mine. (Zena, 30)

I finally understood addictive love and the reason why people stay in abusive relationships. An abusive relationship is better than no relationship at all. We can feel intensity connecting to each other through hurt, anxiety or hate as well as pleasure. My ex-boyfriend's parents drink together, then fight and hit each other and wake up the next morning like nothing happened, except the bruises. How strange, but that's what they do. They are used to each other and they are connected through drinking. They feel that they understand each other. (Carla, 23)

My basic reaction to the passionate experience is to both desire and fear it. I have no real working model of how it works, just the many ways it doesn't. I tend to associate the sexual experience with lack of control, even a kind of insanity. This fills me with fear and dread. In my case, the feeling of where I begin and others end often becomes blurred. The aftermath is a feeling of nonidentity. (Donald, 41)

We didn't have that much in common besides great sex. I would have done anything for him and did almost everything possible. That is why it hurt so bad when it came to an end. (Lily, 20)

He's fun, he's wealthy and he's handsome,
but they've never found his last four wives. . .
Oh well, nobody can be perfect.

Chapter 11

Partner Shopping and the Big But

"The indispensable first step to getting what you want in
this life is this, decide what you want."
— Ben Stein

*There are honest to goodness ways of shopping
for significant others to have in our lives.
Most of the suggestions in this chapter apply
to discovering new friends as well as finding
dates, potential mates or partners.*

The truth is that dating and finding a person who is a good match is hard work. It means putting ourselves out there to meet people in places that seem to attract our kind of person. It also means meeting a number of people who will not work out for us, along with those who have some potential for the future.

When we are dating and sizing up the people we meet as possible mates, this is called shopping. Window shopping comes first as we react to the "outside" of the person based on their appearance, mannerisms, charisma, possessions and apparent status. Sizing them up according to certain other criteria we have is when we get to know them on the "inside," that is, their character, habits, values and personality. This can include a magical process like "I will just know when I meet him" or as Cinderella's "Some day my prince will come. . ." or you can choose a practical process as in "I have my list!"

Remember, your shopping list helps you focus on what you really want. You wouldn't go looking for a car without knowing what it is you want. You wouldn't settle for a car without an engine, and chances are you wouldn't settle for a car that wasn't the style, color or design you want. If you've set your sights on a little sports car, you're not going to be interested in a Jeep, or vice versa.... If you do buy what you don't want, you will be very disappointed and impatient until the day you can trade it in.

If you are shopping in a practical way for a partner, then your list should include the characteristics you want in a healthy relationship. What do you want that to look like? What do you want in your partner? Here are some ideas that other "shoppers" have shared, in no particular order.

- Mutual respect
- Trustworthy
- Good communicator
- Monogamous
- Sense of humor
- Similar values
- Affectionate
- Good self-esteem
- Intelligent
- Has integrity
- Financially sound
- Has clear goals
- Understanding
- Fun to be with
- Unselfish
- Spontaneous
- Independent
- Imaginative
- Secure
- Athletic

- Friendship
- Kissing, holding, touching
- Being in love
- Commitment
- Have things in common

Making Your List

What would be on your list? Begin to think about this and jot down your ideas.

One person made her list filled with specifics and kept it in mind while spending time with a recently widowed friend. The friendship grew and, in time, he became her husband.

She divided her list into two categories: "must have" and "would be nice".

Must have:
- Sparkly eyes
- Smart
- Funny
- Kind and gentle
- 5'7"–6'0" tall
- Good health
- Active/adventurous
- Traveler
- Non-smoker
- Nice hands & face
- Sensuous
- Secure (home, etc.)
- +/- 5–10 years of my age
- Good taste in clothes, etc.
- Likes art, theater, film
- Friendly
- Tidy/organized/clean

Would be nice:

- Golfer
- Reader—literate
- Works part time or retired

On their second anniversary, she revisited her list and was delighted to discover that she had everything on her list in her friend/husband. Her list was specific. Prior to this list, she shopped with a vague notion of hoping to find "someone to love." Even more vague was the hope that things would work out okay.

Your shopping list helps you focus on what you really want. Once you know what you really want, that list stays in the back of your mind until you find a match. It is the model to which everyone is compared. In short, a healthy relationship includes the same characteristics of a healthy friendship.

We modify each other in relationships—we change each other. This is great when we pick up the other person's best traits. However, when a relationship breaks down we think about the positive and negative feelings and experiences that went with it.

When we enter into a relationship with another person, we connect with baggage from our previous experiences, both positive and negative. The baggage we carry encourages us to create revised shopping lists when we are searching for someone new.

If we are in a relationship where there is no sexual energy, probably in the next relationship we will put sexual energy up at the top of the partner-shopping list. If sexual energy was at the top of the list with the last person and that person cheated on you, probably trustworthy will be at the top of our next list.

Our goal in partner shopping may be to fall in love. Falling in love is an experience that repairs wounds. Falling in love is a form of rebirth—we start again with new hope. Everything is new again. Another thing that happens with love is that as we are attracted to someone, we find out more about ourselves. Falling in love with someone else—that merging and changing we do together—brings about an excitement and heightening about ourselves. Life is fun. Being with a new person and rekindling love represents hope and helps us to feel better about ourselves. That is why when we fall in love it's a rebirth and when we fall out of love, or we lose love in some way, we feel a sense of loss of hope.

If you are in a bad relationship, and want out of it, you need to make a new shopping list. The list could include what you don't want as well as what you do want. For example, you might say that your next boyfriend/girlfriend needs to be different. No way will you get involved with someone who loves dogs! It didn't work out. Your emotional conclusion is that the reason it didn't work out is because of the dog, cat or a hobby. Perhaps now you will organize your next list based on new conclusions that you've reached along with your feelings about the previous relationship.

In many of our relationships we give away criteria at the top of our lists dismissing it with, Oh, well, they used to be important, but I can do without that because he is SO cute or so sexy or has such a cute car. From time to time we give away that which is important to us for something that turns out to be really minor over time.

If a monogamous sexual relationship is at the top of your list, then you need to hold out for that. If trust is number one, you need to hold out for that—even if they have money! Money and social status turn many heads away from the planned list. While nice, money and status do not outweigh the high priority items on your partner-shopping list.

Sometimes a female looks at a male and feels that there is potential and begins "training him" or "fixing him." Training him or fixing him means that she has some idealized picture of what the "perfect" person would be like. A careful shopping list would have screened him out in the first place. Besides, maybe he resents being changed.

And what have you taken off your list because you have come to believe that it just isn't practical for you to have it? Or that you are not likely to find it in a person? What part of your dream do you have to kill by taking that item off your list?

ACTION ITEM ·········▶

The List Continues

Now that you're ready to shop, review your list. If it isn't written down, now is the time to put everything you want in writing. Be specific! (Characteristics and traits, lifestyle, interests, religious affiliation or not, night owl or early bird, geographically accessible, age range, career, etc.)

Pick the five items that would be your top five considerations. Prioritize them.

How does this list compare with the one you made in Chapter 2? How would the list be different if made by a young male? A widowed male? A young woman? A divorced woman?

Let's say you are involved with someone and your list has "good communication, friendship and understanding." And their list has "athletic, good sex, and cooks!"

There might be some conflict in expectations, yet both of you say you want a good relationship. Maybe you just need to define your list in a way that the other person understands. What are the similarities and differences? As these are defined, both of you will understand what you are shopping for and not be disappointed.

A good first goal in shopping for a mate is to develop for and in yourself the best qualities on your own wish list. In other words, don't expect to find it in someone else; find it in yourself first. Then look for it and require it in someone else.

But BE what is on your list first; be whatever it is that you value.

Where you shop can determine the selection of eligible candidates to choose from. There will be a difference in the selection at a biker bar, a poetry reading, a church group, a rock concert, online dating and in college classes.

Follow up on your wish list after you go out on a date (first, second or third). Keep it where you can refer to it and do a mental check each time you are with someone of interest. With your list in mind, listen to yourself as you talk with your friends.

No matter how many positive things you report from your list, if you come to the big BUT, you've probably gotten to something that really troubles you.

- But he's a two-time felon
- But she's married — or she's been married five times
- But he's too young/too old
- But she smokes — or doesn't smoke
- But he doesn't make enough money
- But she drinks too much
- But he lives 3000 miles away

Whatever it is that you come to when you're having this conversation — after you say the word BUT, pay attention to what else you say after that. BUT tends to cancel out everything that came before it. The real important stuff comes after the BUT. Pay attention!

When you've identified a big BUT, it's a priority for you. You need to pay attention to it because it bothers you and cannot be overlooked. Some items are non-negotiable for you.

You may say, I can live with this, but if your list included that he have a sense of humor and he doesn't have one, you have to decide if that's a quality item within your top five. If it is a high priority item with you, and that quality is not present, it won't work. If it's a low priority item, then perhaps it's a giveaway.

Remember that if you want a dog but you get a cat, don't get upset when the cat won't bark.

When you hear yourself say BUT, pay attention, no matter how long the positive list is. Your date has everything on your list, BUT — you don't trust her. If you don't trust her, or think she's not trustworthy, the rest of the list doesn't matter.

When you have the conversation with your friend and they ask if there is a BUT...and you can honestly reply that there isn't one, then go for it. This is a relationship of great promise.

When you make your list, be complete in what you want, prioritize it a few times and then shop accordingly. Be patient and hold out for what is on your list. Make a commitment to yourself not to settle for less than what you really want in a relationship.

Although this is a big order, be sure you know who you are and where you want to go *before* you invite someone to share your journey and create togetherness that works!

This is the reassurance I've been looking for, for so long. It has taught me to keep a shopping list and to value my wants and needs and not to sell myself short. What I want now seems so much clearer: I want a relationship to be giving both ways and not one-sided, and I want what I've been giving for so long. My stupid patterns of falling for Mr. Potential are over. I now am starting to understand that for me to love anyone or have anyone love me, I must first love myself. (Danie, 35)

> I married someone very much like my mother and I made up my mind I would please him if it killed me—and it almost did. (Joan, 66)

When I'm honest with myself, I know I am waiting until I'm perfect before I try another passionate relationship. Guess how long I am going to wait? (Donald, 40)

> I have decided to become, to the best of my ability, the type of person that I would like to attract in my life. (Tammy, 35)

I'm amazed to discover that the areas I have found lacking *from* a mate have been the areas I am lacking *to* a mate. I've started working on being the person I want to attract to myself. I've made a list of qualities I feel are important in a mate. Some of these qualities are necessary, some are preferable and some are open for compromise. To do this, I have had to look at the values in my life. I have had to reevaluate all the way down to my core values. (Stella, 38)

> The one thing that I will hold onto for the rest of my life will be "the list". Just recently my boyfriend and I broke up. It was my first real passionate experience and it didn't work out because I now know he was lacking two out of the top five things on my list. I will never ever again date anyone who lacks anything in the top ten of my list. (Dawn, 19)

I don't do this but I know people who make a specific list as an unconscious way of making sure that they never connect with anyone. It seems they take their list to an extreme. How weird is that? (Mary, 23)

> It is important to find a mate that wants the same thing out of a relationship that you do. In order to find that perfect mate and have a successful relationship, we need to find out what we don't want from someone and make sure that the person we are interested in doesn't have those traits. That way we will stay out of bad relationships. (Val, 36)

It's easy to point to a list of ingredients, especially when the list is composed of so many good things that say *I want this* and *I want that* in my relationships. However, people do not come with ingredients labels to tell you if maybe they have something inside that you are allergic to, so you have to go around sampling many of them that interest you, even if it is only because they are different. This process is, of course, dating. Yet I think it is possible that your tastes change over time. I think that there is no such thing as the perfect relationship, just varying degrees of imperfection (perfect would get boring anyway). I agree that you affect and are in turn affected by everyone, so what's right today could be wrong tomorrow. (Nick, 43)

> The one lesson that I will never forget is the BUT lesson. I notice myself saying all the time, He is great but.... or, I like it but... It is so true that once you say BUT the statement previous to the BUT is completely wiped out. There are degrees of BUTS. There can be a small BUT that one can overlook and move past. However, the big BUTS are the ones in which you must really pay attention. (Victoria, 26)

Don't ask for what you don't want. (Kay, 30)

> The qualities that are important to me in a future wife start with her being a good wife to me and a good mother to my children. She is kind, sweet, caring, one who likes to laugh, has a kind heart, beautiful on the inside and on the outside. She is willing to get her hands dirty and doesn't have a problem with

working hard. She needs to be an outgoing, loving, fun person. The ability to cook good food would also be helpful. (Jake, 19)

I want to marry someone with a mutual love for the Lord and who believes that Jesus is his savior. I think that without that foundation I could never be in a successful marriage. (Hannah, 22)

I believe I'm ready for a healthy relationship. I realize that the healthier I am, the better integrated I am, the better the opportunity to draw an equally integrated partner into my life....Oh, I almost forgot, he must be a "toucher"—a hand-holder, a hugger. (Illona, 42)

My list helped me see that things were not going to work out between my girlfriend and me, and this gave me the courage to call it quits. (Quinn, 23)

I know you **think** you heard what I said,
but you don't know what I meant when I said it.
Do you?!!!

Chapter 12

Trusting Versus Trustworthy

"The key is to get to know people and trust them to be who they are. Instead, we trust people to be who we want them to be—and when they're not, we cry."
—Anonymous

There is a difference between trusting, which is something we do, and trustworthy, which is something we are—or are not. The difference can make or break our relationships.

Who is the most trustworthy person in your life? Who do you know that is 100 percent trustworthy and supportive of you, who will tell you the truth even if it's something you don't want to hear? Who in your life do you absolutely trust?

The issue of trust comes up frequently in counseling sessions with my private practice clients. The comments generally focus on the client being a very trusting person. Why, I always wonder, is there so much confusion around the issue of trust and trusting?

It bears repeating that there is a difference between trusting, which is something we do, and trustworthy, which is something we are—or are not. To trust is different than to be trustworthy.

Your View of Trust versus Trustworthy

Think for a moment and write your answers to the following questions in your journal.

▶ Do you consider yourself to be trusting?

▶ Do you consider yourself to be trustworthy?

▶ Have you ever been hurt by someone you trusted? Who? When? Is the depth of hurt based on how much you trusted them?

▶ Have you ever hurt someone who trusted you? Who? When?

▶ If you are a trusting person, can someone take advantage of you?

▶ What does it take to be trustworthy?

▶ Can people trust you some of the time or most of the time, but not always? If you can be trusted only some of the time, are you still trustworthy?

▶ If you lie some of the time and not at other times, how do people know when you are telling the truth?

Remember the quip, "How can you tell when a liar is lying? HIS LIPS ARE MOVING."

We might define trustworthy in a number of different ways.

Many people agree that trustworthy people are:

- always there for you;
- honest;
- aware of your history and still accept you;
- reliable;
- nonjudgmental;
- supportive;
- strong enough to be with you in lots of situations;
- consistent and show up for the relationship again and again;

- centered with a good sense of self and have personal integrity.

Trustworthy people are not perfect because no such perfection exists, but one of their goals in life is to be honest and reliable. The trustworthy people in our lives enrich and nourish us. They help to keep us centered.

Even people who are honest and trustworthy must over time build trust with friends, business relationships, family members and partners. Trust is demonstrated with consistent behavior that builds a history of reliability and concern for others. Telling the truth is part of being trustworthy, as is keeping confidences and behaving in a way that shows an appreciation and valuing of others.

When this trust is demonstrated and reciprocal, a relationship can be solid and will provide safety for the persons involved. Emotional trustworthiness provides a level of comfort that allows us not to have to be on guard or walk on eggshells. You know that feeling of being on guard and it is not a comfortable one.

Do you have the feeling with some of your friends or acquaintances or coworkers that you have to protect yourself from them—even during social times? There are those with the reputation of being a gossip. You know that you need to be on guard with them about what you say because they will repeat everything you have told them, even in confidence.

There are those who will say anything (lie) to impress others or to get ahead in the world.

There are those who will tell you what you want to hear to get what they want from you. And there are those whose goal is to control, not to share. They care more about themselves than they do about you and your feelings.

I find it interesting that one of the issues that seems to bother some of my younger clients most is this: What can you do if you are a trustworthy person, and there is someone who because of his/her background is unwilling or unable to trust you? They ask, "How can I get them to trust me?"

Two possibilities come to mind.

1. They have been so hurt that they cannot trust anymore.
2. They know that they themselves are not trustworthy so they don't trust others either.

My immediate answer would be to say that when you have someone who doesn't trust you, then this relationship isn't going to go very far. But that answer never seems to satisfy the question. Clients want a way to prove that they themselves are trustworthy because they themselves are trusting. Still, that's not the way it works.

What are your choices when someone says they don't trust you? Is it really all "on you" then? Is it your job to prove that they can trust you? Perhaps that is what they want. It shifts responsibility from them to you. In truth, it's not on you. If a person says to you, "I don't trust you," your job is not to prove to them that you are trustworthy. You either are, or you are not trustworthy.

You can ask questions like:

- Have I done anything that has caused you to believe I am not trustworthy?
- Has someone else done something that has caused you not to trust me?

It's about them; it's not about you. You can't change them; you can only change you.

I think when the trust issue comes up, instead of making it your business to show them that you ARE trustworthy so they will change, why not say, "Well, I guess you're going to have to work on this before we can have a relationship." May I suggest that you not commit your life, time and energy to someone who continually asks you to prove yourself?

It troubles me when I see someone devoting their life to dealing with a person who doesn't *do* relationships, or who doesn't trust because they feel no one on the planet is trustworthy (including themselves). Why not say, "You're right." Walk away and find another person; there are others out there who would love to have a relationship with you and who are trustworthy themselves.

And, yes, there are a lot of people in our culture who are not trustworthy. If someone cannot be trusted sexually, can they be trusted at all? What do you think? If you're in a relationship with them, it makes it very difficult to trust them in other areas. Lack of marital fidelity is a major trust issue. If someone is unfaithful to their partner and thinks they'll get away with it this time and it really won't hurt anything, that person begins to organize and live their life around that principle of secrecy and dishonesty. Sexual betrayal can spill over into a lack of trustworthiness in other areas of one's life. If nothing else, they must stay on guard and have an excellent memory or they will get caught. The "where are you?" lies expand to include dishonest answers regarding time, location, other people, energy and money questions. Once you start lying, you keep lying. Yes, your mate does notice. Once caught, the relationship falls apart.

Even the suspicion of betrayal creates a breach between the two people. Is it possible for someone to regain your trust after they have cheated on you? Yes, it's possible—but it's not an easy thing. Forgiveness is an important factor here. All of this takes two people who are willing to do a lot of hard work. Therapy is called for to help the parties work through the behavior and distrust. Betrayal is so damaging to a relationship.

Forgiving and forgetting is not as easy as it sounds; to say you forgive someone after they hurt you deeply is difficult. Forgiveness is not a form of self-sacrifice. It is not about forgetting or accepting the other's behavior. What they did hurt you and it has made a difference in your life and in your relationship. Be careful not to pretend that the betrayal didn't happen. Denial will not help you heal. Forgiveness happens over time and is more than a one-time decision. You choose internally to go on with your life regardless of their behavior. Even if they change their behavior and do everything right from then on, the choice of forgiveness is still an internal one for you to make, or not. I have heard it said that forgiveness is accepting that nothing we do to punish them will heal us. When we forgive, we let go of some intense feelings and try to focus our energy positively on our own lives and futures. This energy is better spent on yourself than continuing to punish those who hurt you. You would be wise not to forget what happened. It hurt.

It is a matter of forgiving but not forgetting. Drain the experience of information so that you learn from it, but don't let it lead you into bitterness. Nelson Mandela took the position that "harboring bitterness and resentment in your life is like drinking poison and expecting your enemy to die."

You have much better things to do with your life. Move on. Make better choices next time. Seek trustworthy people to be in your life. Finding people who are trustworthy can become a time consuming and labor intensive task, but if that's what you want, it is worth the effort. Choosing the right people to be in our lives is not done haphazardly. The theme in this book is to choose carefully, have you noticed?

To illustrate the trustworthy issue in a classroom situation, I wander around the classroom and ask students to consider the following questions.

> ▶ I have a few DUIs, yes, but will you loan me your car?
> ▶ I have a history of stealing but I hear you are looking for a housesitter this weekend. Would you let me do it?
> ▶ Yes, I have lots of bounced checks but would you take a check from me this time?

- I tend to lie a lot but I wouldn't lie to you. You do believe me, don't you?
- I have cheated on my ex but trust me, I won't cheat on you. Okay?
- Historically, I'm terrible at relationships but I would like to have a relationship with you. Will you give me a chance?

Most people are absolutely firm in responding NO to the first five questions and will not take any chances but when it comes to someone terrible at relationships, they willingly say okay, I will give you a chance.

Why is this? Why are we so careful with our possessions and money but so careless with OURSELVES? We gladly risk our feelings, our hearts and our selves with high risk people. Why?

Sometimes when I make this point, the class quietly goes into an "aha" moment of understanding, but there is usually a hard case student who claims to give many chances to people with major relational problems.

I then ask, "Will you give me a five-dollar bill?" Usually they trust me with a bill so I say, "Thank you." As I walk away, I tear it in half and toss it to the floor.

Then I ask for another five-dollar bill from the same person.

"No way, no way," is their response.

I always try several times and then follow up with the question, "Why won't you give me another bill?" They respond with certainty, "Because you would just tear it up again."

"You only allowed me one mistake with the money?" No one in the room could be persuaded to share another five-dollar bill with me.

Once again I ask, "Why are you are so protective of your money, but readily get involved in high-risk relationships?"

One fellow bravely gave me a fifty-dollar bill and dared me. I tore it in half and asked for another.

You see, the issue is not about the trusting nature of the one person but the trustworthiness of the other. If the person is not trustworthy, your trust will not change things. You will be hurt, no matter how trusting you are because it is not about you. It is whether or not the other person is worthy of trust. Period.

Rules to Live By

Rule #1 — Be a trustworthy person.

Rule #2 — Choose other trustworthy people to be in your life.

ACTION ITEM ·········➤

Mapping Your Relationships

Look over your relationship maps and mark those people you believe have demonstrated that they are trustworthy with a T.

In your journal, write your definition of what trustworthy is for you.

Trusting Versus Trustworthy
Bulletin Board

TRUST. . . I learned that I did not have a problem with trust, but I need to be more selective with whom I trust. In the past I trusted someone who was completely UN-trustworthy. (Cammy, 26)

> Concerning the five-dollar-bill lesson, what made an impression on me was not necessarily the ripping up of the bill itself (although, boy, that was funny!), but instead

something that you said. After ripping the person's money in half you made a comment about our trust. You said, "Isn't it funny how UNTRUSTING we are with our POSSESSIONS, yet how TRUSTING we are with people and letting them into our hearts." To me, this is something that I will never forget, because it is so true. Sad, but true, how money, cars, homes—all of these—can be more important and guarded than our hearts. It was a very interesting comment and one that I shall pass on to others. (Nuala, 32)

I know that there must be trust in a relationship but I am so used to having relationships where I don't trust my partner and my partner doesn't trust me. (Tesa, 31)

Sometimes we don't even think twice about letting someone come in and take a hold of our hearts, yet we pause to think about it when it comes to money. That quick lesson made me stop and think about how many times I trusted someone so easily when I really should have put more thought into it. Over and over again I was hurt, but continued to let it happen. The lesson really became real to me when I saw you take the five-dollar bill and rip it in half. When Sharon would not trust you again with more of her money, it made me think why I trusted those closest to me when they hurt me again and again? That was a valuable lesson I learned. (Netty, 29)

I used to keep putting myself out there and getting hurt in the process. I came to believe that nobody is trustworthy. Unfortunately, I still have that belief. I especially have a problem with other females. (Karin, 20)

One of my earliest models was my father. He was the king of making promises and sucked at keeping them. "I'll pick you up at five-thirty on Friday, I promise." "We'll go to Hawaii this summer and make up for missing your birthday, I promise." After instilling all my trust in someone and being let down over and over again, it makes it hard to rely on people. Now I find myself trying not to get too close to people, and looking out for myself a little bit more. (Rose, 20)

Who can you trust if you can't trust the one you love?
(Bonnie, 26)

One of the things that really caught my attention was how all of us are so willing to put our hearts in such terrible positions in relationships. Almost the whole class agreed that if their boyfriend was a liar, they would not trust him and if he had a drinking problem they would not let him borrow their car, or if he had money issues they would not accept a check from him. But yet we were willing to give this guy a chance if he's not real good with relationships, which basically means that he's not real good at sharing and giving his heart and his love to others. Yet all of us were willing to give our hearts and let him take advantage of it in whatever way he wants to. We all had something that we could honestly say about a guy that we did not like, or as Jan would say, we all had a big BUT. And the worst part about our big BUT is that the majority of the class knew before they got involved with this guy that there was something they didn't like, but they just overlooked it. (Bella, 26)

Betrayal is a hell of a wound. (Bill, 60)

Part of taking better care of myself is learning who I can trust to really allow myself to be vulnerable with. A turtle makes no progress until he sticks his head out. I just need to learn how to stick my head out without becoming turtle soup. (Stella, 38)

I used to have gravel friends and fun-house mirrors, until I realized how damaging they were to my spirit. In high school, some part of me always knew that I couldn't trust my best friend, that I wasn't safe with her, but I still hung out with her because I wanted to be accepted by the circle of people that she represented to me. (Kingsley, 44)

My father left when I was ten and I still feel the lack of his being there. When he promises me something, I still go through the stages of grieving when he flakes on me, which is a lot. I am constantly giving him another chance, but now have accepted him for who he is. (Bobbie, 22)

I have decided that I want to be an honest man. (Don, 19)

"When the character of a man is not clear to you, look at his friends."

—Japanese proverb

"Our senses don't deceive us: our judgment does."

—Anonymous

Trusting Versus Trustworthy

What kind of super hero
are you supposed to be?

I'm Daddy.

Chapter 13

I Want To Be Like That

*"Keep away from people who try to belittle your ambitions.
Small people always do that, but the really great make
you feel that you, too, can become great."*
— Mark Twain

***Copying or patterning after others becomes a way
of learning skills and designing our character.
We become like the morsels of others that we
study and practice and claim as our own.***

During a recent visit to the Montage Resort in Laguna Beach, California, I walked across the grounds and looked up at one of the balconies and noticed comedian and TV performer Ellen Degeneres talking on her cell phone. I smiled and waved. After all, I know her don't I? Daily, she and I shared the hour of her TV program while I was in my study working on this book. She smiled dutifully and waved back, without a clue as to who I was, and neither, I am sure, did she care. I was just another fan she had to smile for, and who had in some way invaded her limited privacy.

Ellen is a public person and her private life becomes accessible to us in a way that we probably wouldn't want for ourselves. That is, we wouldn't fancy our lives being so completely public.

Once I dreamt about Oprah Winfrey who is highly recognized and respected all over the world. In my dream, we had dinner together and during the conversation she said she was considering a possible career change. Since I'm a career counselor as well as a therapist, I offered her my professional assistance. In my dream, she said (of all things) that she had a cash shortage because all her funds were tied up. I offered to work something out for her, as I do with all my clients.

Ridiculous? Of course it is. Oprah has no cash shortage and I don't have access to her to visit over a dinner. But for me, the dream was akin to real time and it felt like a real conversation. Oprah was integrated into my reality as she is for millions of viewers. For me, through television, she has an impact on my life even though she doesn't know that I exist.

This false intimacy comes our way every day with all the TV, screen and radio personalities as they visit with us anonymously in our intimate space. We study sports figures and dress by label with the athletes we admire. We time our day by them. We watch them daily or TIVO them into our schedule. We discuss their insights and programs. We follow their careers, watch their games and see their movies. We read the fan magazines and are incensed with the paparazzi for invading their lives, despite our continuing hunger to know more about them. We measure some of our accomplishments by what they are doing and when. ("Yes, that was during the trial of so-and-so that John and I met.") We study their weight and dress. We even dream about them as though they are a real part of our lives.

Why do we do this? It indicates a deep NEED to have people in our lives who we can look up to, admire and emulate. The WHY of this is so that we can learn more about ourselves. We select people, and not only superstars, to look up to, admire and copy because we believe that they are a step ahead of us in some way and they model a quality we wish for ourselves.

As children, we admire our parents, siblings and others who come into our lives because they are able to do things that we can't do. They are taller, older, wiser and more skilled. Maybe they're a few grades ahead of us in school and we wonder if we'll ever be that big or that smart or be able to attain a certain skill. In short, we want their skills and to be like them!

When we're children we select heroes with skills: sports figures, musicians, firemen, soldiers, dancers, movie stars, teachers, (yes, teachers!) coaches, priests, youth ministers, leaders in gangs, tough guys, tall guys, good looking people, and the list goes on, to be the "heroes of our lives" for the moment. We wear t-shirts bearing their pictures or their team name, or number, or their slogan. Again, we want to be like them. In the heat of the hero moments, we want to BE them. We even IDEALIZE THEM.

Idealizing is composed of an *Idea*, the *Ideal* and the development of an *Idol*. When we are in the idealization stage of knowing about someone, we tend to put him or her on a pedestal and think they are bigger than life, or at least bigger than we are. We have ideas about them that are ideals that perhaps we could reach if we live long enough. If we copy them, perhaps we will become smarter, faster, stronger, etc. They become models for us. Taken to the extreme, they become idols.

As we idealize people, we have them in our lives so we can learn from them.

We select a piece of them that is a quality or skill we need to develop in our own life.

When we idealize others, what we do is to locate qualities in them that we wish to own. "I like that, I want to be that." We want to possess something we admire, something that seems ahead of us and outside of our self, far grander than we know ourselves to be YET.

Consider this recollection of a sixty-year-old male.

> During the time of my adolescent years, one of the biggest stars in the movies was James Dean. He was my hero. He seemed to possess qualities that I longed for as a teenager. For instance,

while I was awkward and shy around girls, he appeared to be relaxed and comfortable talking to them. And since I was a rather sensitive person, I could easily identify with the type of roles that James Dean portrayed on the screen. Yet my shyness kept me from being as popular as I wanted to be. I wanted others to be drawn to me much like James Dean experienced. So at some point, I decided that if I could be like him, maybe some of his qualities would rub off on me. I wore similar clothes, I combed my hair like his, I started smoking cigarettes, and I even tried to talk like him. I was cool and confident (at least on the outside!) and I believe that this experience helped stretch me as a person, and it gave me the courage to grow out of my emotional shell.

We want their lives and we want ALL THAT **WE MAKE UP** ABOUT THEM TO BE TRUE.

I emphasize the point that we make up things about them and I say that because of the assumed intimacy that we have with them. However, in truth, we know nothing about them except the part of them that is on display. We don't know what they are like with their families, if they are faithful to their mates, if they are able to be a good friend to someone, if they are trustworthy—these qualities are hidden from us. Because of this hidden quality arena, we make up stuff about them.

If the star quarterback is remarkably skilled at running with a football, then we think he must do other wonderful things too. If the current rock diva is a wonderful singer and dancer, she must be a perfect role model for a teenage wannabe. The most popular kid in school is successful at sports, and we assume that they must also be smart, bright and socially adept in all ways.

If the star of a film gets the perfect mate in the movie, then doing everything that the star does will surely get us the perfect mate. If the admired person is good in one area, they must then, in our minds, be good in all areas.

We copy what we see and what we think we know about them. We learn from them. We incorporate bits and pieces of them into our lives. Young people walk, talk, dress like, and try to think and behave like the people they admire, whether they are peers who are slightly ahead of them or famous people who have riches and fame. They become our heroes and our mentors. To us, they are bigger than real life!

Disappointment, Downfall and Disillusionment

We also are easily disappointed in our heroes when their flaws begin to show. Now why do I tell you all this up front?

When I ask young adults who their heroes are, they are sometimes reluctant to answer, saying they used to have heroes but they don't have them anymore. Pressing further, I find out that it's because they were disappointed by them in some way.

- I used to look up to my father or my brother but they disappointed me.
- I used to look up to that sports star but look at all we learned about him!
- I used to admire the president, but he disappointed us all.
- I used to want to be just like _____, but then something happened and the glow around her went away.

We have both the disappointment *du jour* and yesterday's disappointment. Tomorrow we may have a new hero who enjoys a moment in our sun and then, who knows—it turns out they weren't so perfect after all.

And WE feel let down or diminished in some way. We can feel diminished with and by them when they are flawed or when they fail. We feel perfectly righteous booing them in a crowd or criticizing their performance or discussing their shortcomings with our friends. They were, after all, intimately in our lives through the media, through our belief systems, through what we made up about who they are.

We made up stuff and we feel like we have every right to judge them.

The dilemma is this: When we judge the heroes we have created, we also judge ourselves and we judge what we have incorporated into our lives from them, thus in some ways, disappointing ourselves. Is this perhaps how we lose our enthusiasm? Is this how we become cynical? Is this how we lose the zest to learn and grow?

We can relate this to other questions:

▶ If my hero is Daddy, and he deserts the family, does he take the hero part of me away with him?

▶ If I admire my parent and they withhold their love from me, does it mean I am unlovable?

▶ If people who are great become less great, does that make them losers?

▶ If someone we admire hurts us emotionally, does it make it impossible for us to trust others and to have healthy relationships?

▶ If our hero is ridiculed, are we ridiculed too?

▶ If he or she fails, do we fail too? Is that why we judge them so harshly? Is that why, as we grow, we are reluctant to have heroes and mentors? Is that perhaps why you now feel personally disappointed?

How do we handle our deep feelings about all this?

ACTION ITEM ·········▶

Taking Inventory

List the people who have disappointed you. Who in particular disappointed you the most? Besides their names, list why you admired them and why or how they disappointed you. Is there a pattern here? What can you learn from this? Then make a list of the people in your life who remain positive models for you.

We need heroes and mentors! We need them to help us grow **but we need to be selective about whom we choose and why we choose them as models.** We will benefit the most if we limit our respect to the specific skill areas that inspire us, rather than generalizing about all aspects of their lives.

When you have someone in your life that disappoints you, who you looked up to, remember what it was that you admired about him or her in the first place. If they are **still good** at it, or if they **were good** at that, you can still admire them for that skill. The disappointing aspects are a part of them, too, but the part you selected to admire may still be admirable.

It may come as a surprise to you to know that other people are watching you! You are a role model for someone else. You are a step ahead of someone who is learning from you. Ask yourself:

- ▶ What do you want them to learn from you?
- ▶ What qualities would you hope they would admire?
- ▶ What faults would you prefer they overlook?

I worked with a father who had a quick temper and who couldn't keep it under control in the family setting. He kept his temper in check at work, but not at home. His son studied his every move. By adolescence, the son also had a temper that was out of control.

We are mentors. We need mentors. We are role models. We need role models. But most essential is this: We need to select our models carefully and to be willing to be a healthy model for others.

The Next Step

As we develop, we trade in our heroes and mentors for new ones that will assist us in moving ahead in our lives. We need new role models for the new chapters or new skills that we want to include in our personal portfolio. It's important to know that we can get new models and heroes, particularly if we have been disappointed in a major hero or role model early in our lives.

ACTION ITEM ·········►

Listing Traits

Think for a minute and then write down the names of five or six people who you most admire and respect. They can be real or fictional, historic or family, living or dead. In addition to writing down whom you admire and respect, write down why you respect them. What is it that attracts your attention? What qualities do you think they possess?

What are some of the qualities you came up with?

Samples might be: Strong, fit, peace loving, kind, honest, loyal, has integrity, passionate, patient, powerful, self secure, the best quarterback that ever lived, nonjudgmental, unconditional love, fun, hard working, courageous, intelligent, responsible, embraces life, open-minded, risk-taker, values mutual respect, a true friend, down to earth, a good parent, doesn't compromise what they want out of life, successful, generous, giving.

Think for a minute, who might have some of those qualities? Perhaps you do! Many times, the people we select as heroes have the qualities that we ourselves have, or desire to have. When we make the list of those we admire, the qualities we list are those qualities that actually describe us or the "us" we want to be. They are us; our faith in who we are, and in who we are becoming. These qualities are motivators for us.

Think about the following questions.

▶ From your list, what qualities do you have now?
▶ How much of each quality do you have now—on a scale of one to five? (Five is high.)
▶ What qualities are you missing or wanting?
▶ If you're missing or desiring those qualities, what types of mentors do you need?
▶ Would adding those qualities you desire add to your life?
▶ What kind of people do you need in your life that you can learn from?

Write some of these ideas in your journal.

Who Are the Best Teachers?

While we may be motivated by some negative people or experiences to do things differently, we can learn best from positive examples.

- I want to learn how to be kind from someone who demonstrates kindness.
- I want to learn about relationships from someone who values a healthy family.
- I want to learn about how to be a man from my father or how to be a woman from my mother.
- I want to learn to be honest by admiring someone I know to be trustworthy.
- I want to learn about working hard from someone who takes pride in hard work.
- I want to learn about courage from someone who despite being fearful was courageous anyway.
- I want to teach my children how to choose models wisely so they are not disappointed.
- I want to be a good model for my children because they need me to be healthy and trustworthy of their respect.

- I want to learn about friendships and keeping those friends from someone who is a good friend and who cares about others.
- I want to learn about giving from someone who is generous.
- I want to learn about the place of money in my life from someone who manages money with a healthy perspective.
- I want to learn how to grow spiritually from someone who walks with God and maintains a Monday to Sunday relationship with God.

These very important things I learn from real people who lead real lives. What is it that you most want to learn? Who can you choose to learn this from? Don't try to learn everything at once. Select one goal at a time to focus on and work on that for a month. Focus only on what you want in your life, not on what you don't want.

Selecting and having heroes and mentors in our lives is how we learn and continue to learn to be more of what we wish to be as human participants in relationships. We give back to the world when we become a mentor to someone else.

When we give to others, we help them create togetherness that works too.

ACTION ITEM ········▶

Mapping Your Relationships

Look over your relationship maps and mark an M by anyone who served you as a mentor or as a hero.

My mother was a strong, independent woman. She encouraged
my first uncertain steps into an enlarged awareness of the
world. Her strength and wisdom supported me. "Hitch your
wagon to a star," she would say. "If you only get half way that is
a great distance. But if you hitch your wagon to the outhouse,
you will never leave the yard." She encouraged my dreams and
always felt I could do "it". (Ophelia, 50)

> My parents were not good models, through no fault of their
> own. They inherited "model-nucleosis", not to be confused
> with mononucleosis. It's the disease of poor modeling skills.
> (Queenie, 46)

Am I a role model? I guess I am, because over a hundred kids
look up to me and at times mimic my every move. I never really
thought about being a role model when I started coaching
my neighborhood swim team nine years ago. I was thirteen
when they asked me to help out with the little kids. Now I am
responsible for close to 110 swimmers from five to eighteen
years old. I had no idea that those kids would have such an
effect on my life, nor did I realize how much I would affect
theirs. I like being a role model. I like the responsibility. I like
feeling that I am making a difference. (Aaron, 24)

> As a child I idealized my best friend's family. Her mom and
> dad were happy (her father was not an alcoholic). They had a
> "normal" family environment and I can remember loving to be
> in the midst of it all. I can remember wishing for the same type
> of family for myself. I knew I didn't want to marry anyone like
> my dad. (Elsie, 45)

I cannot help but wonder at all the possibilities we all have in
being shaped. Does some trait of mine come from the family
on "Father Knows Best?" Maybe "Superman?" I have been

very disillusioned by the families I saw on TV as a child. I thought that was the way it really was! Isn't it interesting how contrasting the families are now on TV—from "Married with Children" to reruns of the "Brady Bunch?" (Francie, 50)

> My sister was four years older and I remember vividly how I would see what she was wearing and I would, out of my limited wardrobe, try to copy that day's outfit. She was and is a brilliant, beautiful, sophisticated woman. Simply put, that was how I wanted to be. (Maxine, 41)

This chapter touched me because it reinforced how I want to live. I want to lead a life where happiness is paramount, relationships are real, and love is true. I became aware of my insistence of not being like my parents. Now, instead of focusing on what I don't want to do, I focus on what I do want to do or see in myself. (Inga, 26)

> My mother lived her life totally dependent on my father, and as I am presently trying to adopt a more independent lifestyle myself, I realize how I definitely do not want to be like her. (Bea, 31)

Being a single mother is hard; we know that. I learned the importance of being a good role model to my kids. This could affect their future. I want to become in some way their idol ideal. (Maria, 27)

> I have never felt capable of idealizing anyone. I grew up with the impression that people were not all they were set up to be. I have always been hard on everyone and always been disappointed in those I have looked up to. Now I will try not to expect one person to be perfect in every way. I will allow myself to not always have to try to appear perfect as well. (Olivia, 27)

I have learned to use positivity in my counter-identification with my mother. Instead of saying, "I don't want to be like my mother!" I now say, "I want to be the best mother I can be!" It helps to dilute the bitterness. (Dora, 44)

"A hero is an ordinary individual who finds strength to persevere and endure in spite of overwhelming obstacles."
                                    — Christopher Reeve

I Want to Be Like That

I am unique!

Chapter 14

Belonging and the Rules

"There's a place for us, somewhere a place for us."

—West Side Story

Family rules stay with us, perhaps forever. Changing the groups we belong to and changing values also changes who we are. When we change groups, we change identities. How can this be?

Rules, Myths and Fables

It has been said that we have to live and we have to die; the rest we make up. Along the way, we do the best we can with what we have and with what we believe our life is supposed to be like. Growing up we heard stories about how our life should be.

Some of the stories we heard may include:

- Live happily ever after by getting married.
- Men take care of their women and are rich.
- Work really hard and you will succeed economically.
- If I'm going to be successful, I should have a career that gives me stability and money so I can win the Princess.
- The Princess grows up and her goal is to marry the Prince and be happy ever after.
- Some women are trying to marry a life; men generally are trying to make a life and then marry.
- Females get married to be taken care of.

- Marriage is a good thing, marriage is forever, and love is the fable.

These are myths and fables. We know there is more work to life than the fables express.

The families we grow up in give us *The Rules*, the template, attitudes and values by which we are supposed to evaluate our lives and our relationships. If we are doing what Mom and Dad said was the right way to do it, then we know we are turning out right and being successful. If we do it differently than they taught us, they may say we are doing it wrong. There comes a point where we have to decide what is good for us. This is a big issue.

As children, we were taught what I call The Rules. The purpose of the rules was to teach us how to be successful in the group in which we belonged. In my family, I wanted to be successful. I learned what the rules of surviving and thriving were. I learned how to get by and what to do in order to be really successful in that setting. If I were to have come from another family, their rules may have been different.

One young woman actually wrote down her family rules and came up with ninety-three of them! While family rules usually are not written out, family members know them, from having heard them, or seen them, or been punished over the course of their childhood for not following them. We might identify the rules as tapes that keep running in our heads or the automatic things we do. We wonder, after all, doesn't everyone do it this way?

So we grow up in families where there are rules, written or not, that the family believes and follows. These rules apply to nearly everything.

- There are rules about eating and dinnertime.
- There are rules about family business and the privacy of such.

- There are rules about dating and sex and love.
- There are rules that start "In this family, we…"
- There are rules about chores and who does them, and how.
- There are rules about cleanliness and an agreed upon standard of what's good enough.
- There are rules about religion and politics and other people.
- There are behavioral rules that say, "You know better than that!"

ACTION ITEM ··········▶

Get It Out of Your System!

What are some of the rules you grew up with? Make a list of them. How many rules did you feel you had to rebel against? Write some of these in your journal.

Examples of the rules might be:

- Children are to be seen but not heard.
- If you don't talk about it, there is no problem.
- Cheaters never prosper.
- A penny saved is a penny earned. Save for a rainy day.
- No friends in the house if parents aren't home.
- Homework has to be done before you can play outside.
- Don't play with fire.
- Keep your bedroom door open when you have friends over.
- No noise in the morning; Mom is sleeping.
- Be home by midnight.
- Pee with the lights on, you'll be happy you did in the morning.
- Don't drink until you are twenty-one.
- Clean your plate; think of all the starving children in India.

Belonging and the Rules

- Don't sit on the arm of the couch.
- Don't go to your neighbor's house because you would be a bother.
- If you break it, fix or replace it.
- If you open it, close it.

When you go out into the world, you find that your family rules may be different from those of other families. If you go to a different family, the rules might change and, as they do, you might get a bit confused.

You are trained to behave as a member of whatever social group you were raised in. If your family is involved in a cultural group, you had extended rules there. If they were involved in a church, synagogue or mosque, you had rules there. You behave the way your group told you to behave. That's how you get your start. You say to yourself, if I'm going to be successful, these are the rules.

With couples, rules need to be defined and somehow agreed upon rather than imposed on one person by the other. The difficulty is with unspoken and unwritten rules. There is an assumption that the partner will meet the expectations of even the unspoken rules.

Perhaps the greatest source of stress in a relationship is the assumed belief that the rules are the same for both people. After all, there is a right way and a wrong way to do just about anything, isn't there? Rules are to be followed! Unspoken or not, have you noticed that you can become judgmental about those who do not follow yours? The rules we grew up with are the basis for our assumptions and expectations that lead to judgments, and judgments interfere with togetherness. Being judged by another person never feels good to us.

Why Do I Refer to Them As Rules?

Perhaps the rules started out as guidelines, but along the way they became so ingrained that they hardened into rules.

They carry major expectations with them.

The rules give us clarity about how to be successful in our family. We also learn that in any organization or culture or group, rules or guidelines exist, which, if followed, teach us how to be successful in that group or organization or culture.

Adolescents discover that values and attitudes and certain behaviors that were absolutely unacceptable at home are actually valued somewhere else. At home, if we use a word we're not supposed to use, we may get sent to our room, but if we're out with friends and we say one of those words, they think we're cool. We learn we can use it with them, but not at home, so we learn about *situational ethics*. Sometimes, at home, we might forget where we are and slip and, as a result, we suffer the consequences and are punished.

We could ask senior citizens what groups they were in while in high school and they could tell us all about them. There's a strong identity issue in adolescent groups and, for some reason, the high school group assignment tends to be something we carry with us. We remember if we were popular or not, or if we were looked up to or looked down on. That placement stays with us. The impact is that the high school peer group assignment seems to stay in our consciousness. What group were you in?

As adolescents we try on different behaviors. "This week I'm going to be cool, and what is cool? I'm going to hang out with this group and find out. If I think it's fun, I will keep doing it, or if I find it is not fun, I won't keep doing it. Then maybe I will leave that group." We take on different identities, we dress differently, we identify ourselves differently. We join the drama club. We join the student government. We join the jocks. Each time we want to see if the new group fits us. When we shift groups of people, the rules change too. The goal is to belong.

I had a student who sat silently through most of the class

until we got to this lesson. Then she said, "I finally get it now! This is why I never fit in!" This bright young woman had once been happily attending a private high school. When she had to move to a public high school she felt lost; she didn't fit in. She was in many ways smarter academically than her peers but very young and socially behind them. During this difficult time, her parents divorced. She didn't feel comfortable at home, at school or in the social groups. She tried to fit in and it didn't work. She cut classes a lot and finally dropped out of high school.

Then she took the GED and started college. Academically she could handle college. Emotionally she was not ready to be with older students. She finished a semester and then left for a while. When she returned, she was much more mature and a little more settled and that's when she took my relationship class. When we got to this lesson, Belonging and the Rules, she said, "I finally fit somewhere!" She shared with the class her earlier disconnect and that happily she finally felt that she belonged.

At the end of the semester she was ready to graduate and, sadly, she was killed in an automobile accident. I never think about Belonging and The Rules without remembering her with affection and fondness. She really brought home to each and every one of us how personal this issue is. I miss her.

When we belong somewhere, we have an identity. Understanding the rules helps us to fit in and to belong. Belonging is related to the rules of the group, spoken or not.

If there doesn't seem to be a place for us and we don't feel like we belong or feel comfortable in our own skin, then it doesn't matter that we are doing well or achieving. Emotionally, we are still left out.

It is also a way we define ourselves. If I'm feeling like I don't belong or fit in anywhere, I could join a group that shares interests that I have or that I want to develop. As soon as I've joined, I could say to you, "I'm a member of such and such a group." This could be a service club, social group, political party, sports group or any other group that has some kind of recognizable purpose.

Groups and Belonging

There is an advantage when you belong in a social group. The advantage is that you feel included and probably share some interests in that group. When you belong to the Sierra Club, you are with others who like being outside and going for a hike. When you belong to the PTA you are with other parents who share similar interests or concerns with you. When you join a social group that likes to dance or go to dinner, it's a place where you share activities and are included. When you join a gym or athletic team, you get to be with others who are developing similar skills.

Sometimes when you join a group, you give up a bit of your individuality in order to belong. Some of your rules may be in conflict with theirs. For example, if you join the military, you give up your individuality in terms of hairstyle, dress and decision making. When the commanding officer orders you to do certain things, it is not acceptable for you to say, "I don't want to, or I have a way to improve this." You are to look like everyone else, march like everyone else and behave like everyone else—because that is what makes the military work. The military, in order to be successful, has a group of rules and a chain of command, which must be followed, and followed immediately, exactly and completely.

In gang membership, the rules may be somewhat the same. Members will dress a certain way to identify membership in their group. If they dress another way they might be identified differently and they are liable to get hurt. They will behave and talk a certain way because they are expected to represent the gang's "culture."

In corporations you may give up your individuality and learn the corporate culture of behavior and dress so you can be successful within their culture.

In an Amish community they probably wouldn't let you bring along your computer or cell phone.

In a private school, you may be required to give up your own style of dress and wear a uniform.

In jail, you have to give up freedom, good food, all the stuff in your pockets, and wear a bright orange or blue uniform, even if the color is not good on you.

Living in a strong conservative/traditional Arab culture versus a liberal one in San Francisco would be a culture shock, particularly for a woman. If you take up riding a Harley Davidson and hang out with other bikers, you'll begin to be identified with the biker group, whether you are inside the group or not. You become identified with the group you are seen with. Even if you are only a weekend biker, when you wear the uniform, or behave a certain way or are seen in a particular place, people assume (rightly or wrongly) that you share the characteristics of that group. You are like them in others' eyes.

If you make a lifestyle change, you may find that you have shifted groups, and at the same time, shifted rules. If you decide you want to go to college and the people you have been hanging out with surf all day, it's probably not the group that is compatible with you, because they will want to go surfing instead of studying and that will not help you get good grades.

If you decide you want to be drug free, you need to leave a group that uses drugs and not behave that way anymore. If you try to hang out with them, you probably will be tempted to do drugs again. It's your choice; hang out with people who are not using, or people who do. Few people can blend membership in both groups and still stay clean and sober.

If you get divorced or become a widow/widower, you are

in between groups. Your connections with couples change dramatically.

When you have children and your single friends want to go out, they may not understand that you can't just leave the children and walk off.

Change and the Impact on Togetherness

Getting married is a time of great identity change. There is a big shift. When you first get married, it means leaving the single life and joining a total new lifestyle. It may include a mother- and/or father-in- law. What are the new rules? And do you need to continue following your old ones as well? What about single friends? How do you hang out together when you are now married? How do the time demands of having a part-ner change your availability? Maybe you shift to another group of parents and you have single or married friends who do or do not have children.

If there is a loss of an important attachment, or "break up," there is a shift in identity. After a break-up, belonging is a big issue because, socially, we used to share certain people and places together. Now, who gets custody of that particular place, and the home or apartment, or our favorite places and friendship groups? What are the new rules?

When a major holiday comes up like Thanksgiving, you're probably not invited to your ex's family sit-down dinner. The kids also have to decide if they go with Mom or Dad or split up. It is not just a matter of you and your partner breaking up; it includes many people besides the two of you. It has a ripple effect and makes changes in all other relationships as well. Have you lost a family because of the divorce? Now you may have to create a new place and group to share holidays with.

One of my friends, who was unhappy with his wife, put it to me like this: "Can you imagine, she wants to go out and find herself and go back to school and get a career? I didn't marry her for that." He was unhappy with her because she was changing and he wanted her to remain as she was. They subsequently divorced, and it was a change in our social group as she and he went through their mid-life crises. They both began to search for another partner and group. Regarding an approaching holiday, he said, "What am I supposed to do? She's the mother of my children and she is supposed to fix Thanksgiving dinner. She is supposed to be at home and do these things." That was his image. Those were his rules. She had broken them.

She said, "Not anymore. The kids are grown and I am out of here." He didn't know how to cook, do the laundry, etc. It was time for him to learn those things, which he didn't like at all. She and he both started to date, and he would ask me what to do when you date. She would be dating and call me and ask what to do when you date. It is interesting to be in the middle of divorcing friends, isn't it? It is also challenging to start over and learn new skills of functioning after a divorce.

The death of someone close to us changes the structure of our lives very quickly. With an illness or handicap, the whole family unit might be visiting the hospital or rearranging their lives around that. A lifestyle change may happen. Loss of a job would be a huge change. Retirement and loss of children (when they leave the nest) requires life changes and adjustments. The empty nester might ask, "Who am I now if I'm not fixing lunches and taking care of the kids?"

Things in our lives change as our lifestyles change.

If you join a new group, you gain a whole new sense of belonging and a whole new group of friends or acquaintances. There will be new rituals and maybe new ways of having fun. This is the adventure of change.

Adolescents hang out with people whose behavior and appearance is incomprehensible to their parents. Our parents say, "They are not like us; they don't dress like us, they don't talk the same, they don't have the same values." But we think they are cool; we hang out with them. Our parents look at us in amazement.

Later on, adolescents look at their parents' friends and want to ask them the same question, "Why do you hang out with them? They are weird." We have a tendency to evaluate our parent's groups, and our parents are evaluating us; we just do it differently, but we are all looking for PLUs, people like us, with rules like ours so that we can belong.

What is the most important thing to an adolescent? To belong and to fit in. They want to dress the right way with the right labels and the right brand, as if these are rules (and in a sense, they are).

As we get older, we all still want to belong. When we get a new job, we want to belong there or at least with some part of the group that is there. When we are in a class, we want to belong or to fit. When we move to a new neighborhood, we want to be welcomed and accepted. It's a terrible thing not to belong anywhere. The rules are the key. The values of the group set the rules. Your values have to mesh with the group's values or you will not want to follow the rules.

Sexuality and the Rules

One of the heaviest of the rules has to do with sexuality. We learn through our family, religion and culture, when we can have sex, how we can have sex and with whom. There are very specific rules about all of it. In Chapter 10 on sexuality, I asked you what your family rules were about sex. Perhaps you responded "not having sex until you were married" although perhaps you did not follow that rule.

Answers to when it is acceptable for you to have sex might be when you are married, old enough to be responsible for the outcome, when you are in a committed and caring relationship or after you really get to know someone.

To the question, What kind of person can we experience

sex with?, your answer might be someone I love, someone who respects me, someone who meets the criteria on my list or, perhaps, someone who has a job! There are rules about who we should be with, and when.

There is another set of rules about marriage. Depending on where you grew up, whom you marry may be a huge concern. I had a student who had a wonderful boyfriend and wanted to get married, but in her culture the first born had to get married before any other children could get married. She said her older sister was "unfortunate looking." The possibilities for my student to marry didn't look good because, according to their family rules, her sister had to get married first.

There are also cultures that arrange marriages. Suppose your family has arranged a husband or a wife for you? The date is set and your family will be paid well for you. How would you feel about that? Not good? Here in this culture, you can say no, but in other cultures you cannot.

I have a colleague I enjoy very much who tells me stories about growing up in Iran. Her grandmother was married at age nine, to someone in his forties, and she had her first child at age eleven. In our culture, we would consider it child abuse, rape, and illegal. The grandmother at nine had no choice. Yet, within their culture, it was considered normal and acceptable.

If you were a female growing up in Iran at that time, you could be married off at nine or ten and you wouldn't have the advantage of maturing sexually, making choices and finding out who you are. You would be assigned a husband. Your life would be about being his wife and mother to his children. That would be your identity for the rest of your life because divorce is not possible for women in the culture. Men could choose to divorce but women could not.

The areas of sexuality, marriage and divorce become a major concern. If you belong to a certain religion you cannot divorce, or if your partner is not of the same religion, you cannot be married in the church or temple, because those are the rules.

There are rules about how to view our relationships inside and outside of the family. How many of you heard: "This stays within this house; don't talk about this, as this is family business." Or, "we can talk about that here, but don't talk about it with anyone else." (Then we go out and share it with our best friend!)

ACTION ITEM ·········▶

Adjusting to Change

Make a list of the major changes in your life so far. Did the changes involve joining a new group(s)? Did you notice any new rules? What were they? How long did it take before you felt like you belonged in the new group(s)?

Cultural Cutlery

Are you familiar with the British style of eating? They manipulate the silverware differently, putting the food on the back of the fork, which is held inverted in the left hand instead of on the front of the fork. I traveled in England for a while with someone I enjoyed very much. I learned how to eat their way despite the fact that I stabbed myself in the mouth a lot. English people would eat so fast. The food was hotter and they just slipped it on the back of the fork and then quickly into their mouths. I was always the last one finished.

At Thanksgiving that year, when I returned home, I was putting my food on the back of my fork and became aware the entire family had become quiet. I asked what was wrong, and my mother said, "What are you doing, Janet?" (I knew I was in trouble.) I told her I was eating. She asked why I was doing it that way, and I said it was what I had learned when in England. I explained that it was the way the English eat. She promptly told me, "We don't eat that way here." So I tried to show her the efficiencies of it, and she repeated, "We don't eat that way here!"

When my friend John visited from England, he began eating a hamburger with a fork. I demonstrated to him how we grab that burger with our hands and stuff it in our face. He exclaimed, "That's uncivilized." We had a big fight because… it involved the rules. Rules may involve how you use a fork. If you don't do it right, you are in trouble.

While our groups make demands on us, in exchange they hold us together. "If we play by the rules, our family will support us." "If we play by the rules, our church, colleagues, employers will support us." "If you do it differently, they may not support you, and you may have to move to a different group." Being ostracized from a group for breaking the rules can be traumatic. Losing your membership in a group or family can leave you feeling lost and alone.

For the individual without a group, or who is in between groups and really doesn't have a place, there can be an experience of meaninglessness and isolation. One might compare this meaninglessness or collapse of a social structure to the collapse of a bombed building. When it collapses in on itself, there is little or nothing that remains except rubble. People going through a divorce identify with this feeling and this picture.

Anton Boisen was a patient in a mental institution who wrote himself "sane" through a process of self inquiry. He discovered that when we are in between structures or relationships or even realities, this is the time when we are "insane." Landing on another reality, or finding a new structure, new group or relationship can repair that which has been wounded and sanity can once again be a part of our lives. His later work as a clinician, following his experience as a patient, opened new thinking in psychotherapy and pastoral counseling. For him, relationships were the keys to unlocking mental health. For you, successful relationships can enhance your mental and physical health.

The Rules and Connecting

I must confess that I have a selfish reason for writing this book. I believe that when you learn about all of the elements that help make up a healthy relationship, you will be able to use this information to make your relationships healthier. Perhaps the people you choose as friends will be different. Choices you make can help your children make healthier friendship and dating choices. When that happens, I will be connected in some way to you, your unborn children and to their unborn children, and this book will have made a difference.

Who you choose to spend time with sets the rules. Rules of kindness, respect, trustworthiness, fidelity, family values, etc. directly impact the quality of our togetherness.

The decisions that you are making today are going to impact your future and the future of the people you are involved with. The ripple effect may be considerably larger. It's worth it to make good choices!

ACTION ITEM ··········▶

Mapping Your Relationships

As you review your relationship maps, note the people or groups who set the rules for you at different times in your life. Mark their circle with an R.

Write in your journal about the impact of the most important group in your life.

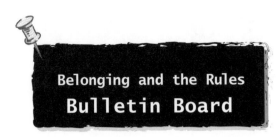
I grew up caught between eastern and western cultures and that has affected my life and my choices. I am still at a stage where I realize I am more comfortable with western culture and yet I have not completely left behind the values and ideas shaped from eastern culture. I am aware of how this clash of cultures is also a contributing factor to the fact that I have yet not been able to feel comfortable about going ahead with a divorce. (Bee, 31)

> Popularity is not as important as our culture makes it out to be. It is embedded in me that I need to look a certain way and act a certain way, but I realize now that I sure as heck would rather be me with all my faults than a hot chick with a fourth grade vocabulary and a negative budget from buying trendy clothes. (Karussam, 23)

I feel more comfortable with disabled students because I don't have to explain my speech problems, my inability to focus when overstimulated, and my nervousness in large groups of people. Most of these students have great listening skills, wonderful humor and a special quality that words don't justify. I belong with them because of my own learning disabilities. This semester was especially difficult for me dealing with agoraphobia, my mother's death and returning to school. Important people in my life agree that college was a lifesaver. (Emma, 36)

> Most of my life I have felt a tremendous split in myself between being a Christian and being gay. No one could see the conflict and pain that flickered beneath the polished surface I presented. After college I became unwilling to forego my own nature in order to please others and did not want to be hypocritical so I embraced being gay. Reconciling one to the other has been frustrating and seemingly impossible from

either side. The inability to reconcile these two parts of me has led to a lifelong struggle and made it impossible for me to find peace. Christians saw my faith and spiritual desire and could not understand my homosexuality. My gay friends saw my comfort and openness with my sexuality but could not understand my deep spiritual connection. (Rick, 39)

Boys and young men have a tremendous pressure to conform to the hypothetical "real man." Real men don't cry, we are told, but those same people who are telling us this may be beating their wives or having affairs. I personally agree with Kurt Cobain, "When I learn to cry I'm a man." (Rafe, 25)

I moved my family from an unsafe neighborhood filled with gangs to a safer community here in Southern California. We now have a home here. We have fun here and we have so many new friends. We walk our dog in the neighborhood and our children run free and play with their friends. We feel safe here and we finally belong. I no longer want to be a part of the old party scene. I belong in this family neighborhood community. (Isaac, 47)

"If you must play, decide on three things at the start: the rules of the game, the stakes, and the quitting time."

—Chinese Proverb

Chapter 15

The Richness of Togetherness

"Close friends . . . contribute to our personal pleasure, making the music sound sweeter, the wine taste richer, laughter ring louder because they are there."
— Judith Viorst

Sharing experiences and events with special others contributes to the richness of living. We need others in our lives, and this allows us to learn more about ourselves. We find our friends and soul mates through sharing fully with another.

219

In today's world, more and more people experience lives of isolation and insulation, brought about in part by our cyberspace connections. The Internet and e-mail have the potential to connect us to each other and yet we are actually cut off from social interaction because of it. How do young people learn social skills when they spend so much time at the computer while they could be interacting with their family and friends face to face?

Cyberspace has instant connections. The question is, "Who are we really connecting with?" Online identities can be assumed and changed in a flash. Are we e-mailing a child, an older man, a married woman, a convict in prison? Who knows! While delightful connections can be made, dangers also lurk with cyber-predators many times taking advantage of the technologically naïve. Connecting with others, without the protection of introductions and recommendations by trusted friends, can lead to disappointment at best and, in some cases, it can lead to danger. Some research has been done which says that people feel even more isolated when they experience the emptiness of discussion groups and chat rooms online because of the anonymousness of the connection.

Friendship is a critical need for all of us. Without contact with friends, we can experience deep loneliness. One company in Germany became a hit when it offered wallpaper that had life-size pictures of ordinary looking people in everyday poses sitting on a couch or standing in the room of their choosing. Each "fake friend" pictured on the wallpaper is well groomed and realistic and, although not very talkative, promises to "be there" and allow the "roommate" to feel not so alone. The company even promises to provide custom wallpaper of "your" mate. If your mate travels a lot you will not miss their presence quite so much! Check out the site at http://www.berlintapete. de/dbtapete/shopcard.php?142

Teenagers (and adults) enthusiastically play "The Sims", a computerized strategy game that allows players to create a family of virtual people and to control those people as they grow up, get married, have kids, grow old and eventually pass on. I was introduced to this remarkable program by Julie, a bright eighth grader, who explained in a flurry that "it had lots of cool stuff—like you can get a job to earn money, and if your pet dies, you get a little grave and you can mourn by it; you can even kiss a boyfriend that you create." She explained that it was important to let the virtual people have a bathroom break because if you didn't, they would pee in their pants and make a mess. A little vacuum then shows up and you have to clean the carpet. Further, she added, "If you have kids and don't take care of them, someone comes to take them away and if you miss work two days in a row, you lose your job!" The game allows young people an advanced version of family life education that teaches them to build and customize homes, keep the Sims happy and learn family dynamics while experiencing the outcomes of a variety of behaviors. In effect, they control the virtual life of the Sims.

http://thesims.ea.com/us/index.html

But let's look at real life.

Friendship Is a Skill

Do you have the friends you desire in your life? Isn't it interesting that some people have lots of friends and that some people have none? If you want to learn about friendship, watch what people do who have lots of friends. I think you will see that they listen to others, appreciate and like others, and stay in touch and connected with their friends.

If you are someone who doesn't have friends—or as many good friends as you'd like—then perhaps some tips might help you.

Friendship Tips

First of all, you must be the kind of friend you want to have. I think, at the acquaintance level, persons **do** together in order to **be** together. That is, they share activities that they enjoy and this in turn leads to talking together about interests, feelings and personal history. Togetherness doesn't happen all at once. It happens over time, which allows a shared history to develop.

Friendship is about trust, sharing, risking together, doing things together that you enjoy and feeling safe enough together that you can just be yourself. The risking is done a little bit at a time. People who dump their entire histories on you at the first meeting can be high maintenance connections. Choose carefully those with whom you wish to really share yourself. There is a kind of equality in friendship that needs to stay balanced. Both must share and listen in alternate rhythms.

Do you have different kinds of friends to meet the many needs you have for social interaction?

I say "different kinds of friends" because we need different people to meet different needs. It's a mistake to expect one friend or a mate to meet all our individual needs. One person probably cannot do it successfully anyway. Humans are needy people. Needs are a normal condition, not a negative. We need others to be in our lives. A variety of acquaintances helps us to be balanced and not overburden those close to us.

What Are Different Needs of Friendship?

Friendships might include those with whom we play, casual dating friends, friends who are funny, shopping partners, mall walkers, travel pals, e-mail friends, garage sale buddies, friends who are serious, church friends, spiritual partners, book club friends, and those who are friends for casual events like watching sports, shooting hoops or playing softball. Then there are those special few we want in our lives for all time. They may be called buddies, pals, chums, friends or soul mates. Whatever we call them, they enhance and brighten up our everyday lives. We all need friends.

ACTION ITEM ··········▶

Defining Friendships

Who are the people in your life that you go to when looking for a good laugh? Who do you go to when you need advice? Who do you feel closest to? Name three people who you like to be with. Write these names in your journal.

The Circle of Friends

The variety of connections can be explained with a circle of friendship—layers that lead to an intimate inner circle. At the innermost core is a trusted and trustworthy group of those we call intimate friends.

The outer core of our circle of friends might be the people we encounter in a casual way, that we enjoy briefly, or that we have just met. They might be persons we decide to screen out of our personal life. They would be acquaintances.

A next layer of the circle might be those we work with or those we have contact with on a somewhat regular basis. They might be our neighbors. Some we enjoy and others we do not.

Perhaps the next level is a group with whom we play or recreate. We spend more time with them in a spirit of teamwork or fun. We share a level of enjoyment and become friends in that way.

Those with whom we share other activities might be the next ring of the circle. Perhaps other parents or classmates or teammates that we know well, with whom we share ups and downs, would be in this group.

Circle of Friendship

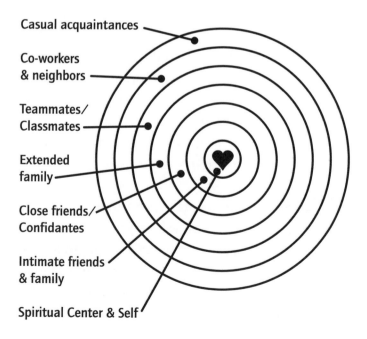

Casual acquaintances

Co-workers
& neighbors

Teammates/
Classmates

Extended
family

Close friends/
Confidantes

Intimate friends
& family

Spiritual Center & Self

Our extended family, parents, aunts, uncles, adopted or by birth, cousins, grandparents and siblings can be a source of closeness or dysfunction. For each person that has the joy of a healthy family there are no doubt an equal number of people who have the pain or difficulties of a not so healthy family.

Those who share joy, also share closeness. The closeness allows us to let down our guard and feel safe. Those who share dysfunction must learn to protect themselves from assumed but false intimacy, which can lead to deep hurts. The deep hurt comes from wishing it were different and letting down any safety guards. Dropping your guard leads to disappointments when the family or family member continues to behave the way that was hurtful to you in the first place. If you have experienced this kind of hurt, I recommend that you change the name from "family member" to "adult relative." It helps to put some distance between you.

There is a circle of close friends and confidants, those with whom we comfortably share ourselves — our real selves. They have been in our lives for the test of time. The relationship has lasted.

At the innermost center or core is the immediate family or one's mate or a best friend, or significant other, one's trusted pet, or one's children. At the center can be our connection with God or a spiritual belief. At this center are relationships that protect us and for whom we provide protection. It is a group that reflects a shared history and a decision to care for each other.

Many people make the mistake of meeting people casually and then invite them almost immediately from the casual outer ring into their inner core in an attempt to establish instant intimacy. This shortcut is fraught with disappointment and disenchantment. It doesn't work and it doesn't last. It is not about real friendship. It is usually about major disappointment.

Real friendship is created over time and usually takes several years to be established. It takes an investment of time to connect with other people. It is cleverly put by humorist Alf Whit when he says "I know that somewhere in the Universe exists my perfect soul mate—but looking for her is much more difficult than just staying at home and ordering another pizza."

There are some persons who remain friendless because they don't learn the skills of friendship in the developmental years of their lives.

Cyberspace and games like the Sims and other virtual realities provide substitutions for the high quality connections they could have with real friends and acquaintances. The substitution works but not like the personal interaction of togetherness with someone whose physical company you really enjoy.

Resonating

Have you ever looked across the room at a friend, connected with their eyes, and without a word understood what the other person had in mind? Many times you both burst out laughing. Not a word was spoken, but across the room, with your eyes, you connected. This energy and messaging (and you did not mistake the message) has to do with resonance.

You can have a mutual experience, although a mutual experience does not equal resonating. Let me give you an example. When Lily Tomlin performed her one-person play, *The Search for Signs of Intelligent Life in the Universe*, in Los Angeles years ago, I called a friend and invited her to go with me. We drove over an hour to attend. Tomlin was wonderful (in my opinion) and everyone in the auditorium was experiencing the same emotions of the play and shared laughing and crying, depending on the content. We were sitting in the dark and yet, I had the sensation that my friend wasn't *getting it*. There was lack of energy and lack of participation, which I just *felt*. I asked if she was enjoying the play. She said she thought it was okay but didn't speak with any energy about it. In contrast, I thought it was a brilliant performance.

When I became aware that the person I was with didn't like it and was bored, it ruined the performance for me. When the play was over, we drove home with a total disconnect. I was upset that the performance that I valued had not been shared.

When I got home, I called another friend known for her wry sense of humor and invited her to go back with me to see the play again. The performance, with this friend, led to great enjoyment and the resonating of the experience. She enjoyed it as much as I enjoyed it. We enjoyed it *together!*

ACTION ITEM ·········➤

Uneventful Event

Have you gone somewhere with someone who did not enjoy the event or experience as you did?

How did that affect the experience for you? Make some notes for yourself. Perhaps you would like to describe those feelings in your journal.

Mutual, that is, being in the same place and doing the same thing with another person, does not necessarily make for a sameness of experience. In other words, you can both be attending an event together which one person loves and another hates. You have experiences different from each other's. Resonating means you are experiencing something in similar way with another person.

If I'm alone watching a sunset and it's beautiful, I might remark to a stranger how beautiful it is because I want to share it with someone. Energy is palpable; we can feel it. The experience is fuller when it is echoed in another. It's a lot more fun to have an experience with someone. This doesn't mean we can't have an experience alone and have it be valuable. Absolutely, we can. However, if you are with someone who is enjoying the experience equally, it becomes bigger because you are sharing it. Like the proverbial fish story—every time fishing buddies tell others how big the fish was that got away, the fish gets bigger and bigger!

Being "Tuned In"

Me, you, or us are three different spaces we can be in. If I am into *me* right now, it's hard for me to be into *you*, or into *us*. That's not where my heart or mind or attention is right then. My focus is on other things.

Sometimes we are very much tuned in to others. We sense things from them because of our closeness and because of shared experiences.

If a friend of yours walked in the door you might be able to tell if they were upset without a word being spoken. Often you will sense someone is troubled and you will ask them, and they say everything is fine, but you know that it's not fine.

We continue to be aware of this non-verbal behavior and we communicate wordlessly what is difficult to put into words and we understand the things we see that are beyond words. I cannot tell you how I know, but I know and I know that I know.

Have you ever just *known* something or *sensed* something without any information to support it? We call this intuition. When it comes to sensing things about people you meet, nine times out of ten you'll probably be right. Trust yourself. We are talking about reading something that is coming across the room as energy. How many times have you looked back on a relationship and secretly confided to yourself, "I knew that when I first met him/her?"

Intuition is a way of knowing without measurable evidence. Intuition is with us when we are infants, before we have language, and it continues throughout our lives. We know it, we feel it and we communicate wordlessly. This is from the part of us that does our deep communicating. It is particularly strong with people who are in our inner circle or inner core of relationships.

When comparing men and women, women tend to have a lot of friends and they tend to talk to their friends as confidantes, and share their feelings and experiences. Men tend to share emotionally with their mate rather than with their male friends. This is changing somewhat and men are starting to share their feelings with other men, however, they still feel the safest only sharing their feelings with their spouse.

Listening

Do you remember an instance of talking on the phone when you sensed the person you were talking to wasn't listening to you? How did you know? Perhaps you heard other activity behind them or they were responding with short answers. There was something empty in their replies.

Whether it's on the phone or in person, we know when someone is really listening to us and is *with us*. When they are listening to us, we call that "resonating" because there is an enthusiasm and energy around the conversation.

Have you ever been with someone and noticed that while they were looking at you and smiling as you talk to them, you knew they were somewhere else and were not hearing a word you said? Or perhaps they were listening and they didn't care. There is a difference between those who are listening politely, and those who are really listening, even though from the outside it may look somewhat the same.

On the other hand, one of the things that happens after you and a friend share an experience is that when you talk about it, you're both talking and enthusiastically involved in the conversation. You can hardly get the words out fast enough. You start laughing, and remembering things and you're excited. When that happens, both people are totally present and wrapped up in what is being talked about. The listening is from the ears, the brain and the heart.

I once heard: "You should have seen that guy listen! I could tell that he was fully involved with what was being said." What a compliment. Listening is not easy work; it takes a lot of energy. You're a good listener when you are fully present and tuned in to the speaker.

Twinship

When someone is fully present with us and they are close friends, we might say we have a soul mate. We have someone who is so close to us that they understand us, often without words. We have achieved Aristotle's paradigm of friendship which is "a single soul dwelling in two bodies." They are so close that they understand our feelings.

One of the best examples of a single soul dwelling in two bodies is the case of identical twins. My mother was an identical twin. Growing up, the twins got into a lot of mischief, had a lot of fun, and sensed what each was thinking and doing most of the time.

Identical twins come from one egg that is divided, so there is a cellular level connection. The connection was so strong with the two of them that if one was sick, the other felt it. My mother and her twin sister had a double wedding with twin bridesmaids. Then after they got married they lived in two apartments, up and down from each other. Later, they built two identical houses next door to each other with a reverse plan so that my mother and her sister could wave at each other through the kitchen windows while they were cooking.

When I grew up, I thought everyone had two mothers and two fathers because that's what I had. Although I was the first-born in my family, I was the second born in this bigger family because my male cousin was the elder. Here I was, thinking that everyone has two mothers and fathers, and mothers who look alike. That's not entirely true, but if you think I'm a little strange, it's because I come from a strange but fun family situation.

My mother and her twin sister remained identical, even at age eighty-seven. They still giggled alike; they even bought the same thing at different stores when they shopped separately.

When they were younger, they both worked in banks in Los Angeles and at lunchtime they would get together to eat.

Once, my mother went out to meet her sister for lunch and she wasn't there. Suddenly my mother got very ill. She left work and went home. When she went upstairs to where her twin was, she asked, "Why didn't you tell me you were pregnant?" My mother was experiencing morning sickness, and it was her sister who was pregnant!

When her sister was quite ill and had gone through surgery my mother was awakened from a sound sleep and became ill, and remained that way throughout the morning. She tried to call her sister and couldn't get through initially, but later reached her and learned that her twin had gotten ill in the middle of the night. It had awakened my mother from a sound sleep and she shared the sensation of being ill as well.

The good news is that they had had a lot of fun and sharing together. Her twin sister died in February, and my mother followed her in May of the same year, just ten days short of their eighty-eighth birthday.

I always thought it would be great fun to have a twin. This speaks of my deep longing for one who is totally resonant. This person would know me so well that they would be with me no matter what happened.

Have you longed for someone like that?

In the search for meaningful friendship, each of us wants someone in our lives who is so close to us and understands us so deeply that we don't have to explain a lot of what is going on inside us. We in turn return the favor.

When we find someone with whom we really resonate and with whom the communication is very clear, it is the highest connection of friendship.

A soul mate is a friend, someone with whom we have on-going closeness and resonating experiences. Friendship is the "we", and we have created this entity ourselves. There are no two other relationships that will ever be the "we" that you and I have; we have created something that is uniquely ours.

As close friends, we use a shorthand form of communication. We have been together and are familiar enough with each other that we don't have to use a lot of words to explain ourselves. We can just start a sentence and the other one knows the rest of it. That doesn't mean that people don't sometimes finish our sentences incorrectly.

Friends or soul mates with whom we have ongoing close-ness tend to use fewer words. We know what they are feeling and talking about.

The Inevitable Challenge

When we have a relationship that lasts over time, some-times we feel really close to the person and want to tell them everything that's on our mind, and sometimes we withdraw and just want to be into *ourselves* for while.

We alternately participate and shift back and forth between the *me* and the *you* and then the *we*. This involves trusting and having the confidence that when I trust myself with you, and when you trust yourself with me, that we have created a *we* that we respect and value so very much, that we will always protect it. We are very concerned with keeping the *we* that we have created as something special.

Ideally, we would like our spouse to be our best friend, but sometimes that happens and sometimes it doesn't. A spouse fills the intimacy place in a special way and the nights are shared exclusively with them. A best friend can be someone who has been with us since childhood and shares a history of other experiences. They occupy a place no one else can take.

One major issue in close relationships is how much *me* and how much *we* will be shared. It's often a stress point in a relationship because one person may want to be alone or be unable to share a great deal at the time, and the other may begin to think s/he doesn't love me anymore. Sometimes one person may be tired or have other priorities. It creates tension but it is part of negotiating how much *we*, and how much *me*.

"This isn't against you; it is for me," is a phrase I often use when there is a need for separate time rather than *we* time.

Another problem can be that despite the closeness, there comes a time of parting. Perhaps you have been best friends for many years and all of a sudden one of you is going away. Maybe you are leaving for school, getting married or raising children. The different explorations of the world which each of us are doing can get on a collision course. We've had all these years of feeling close to each other and suddenly it feels like our relationship is changing. Perhaps the people we are attached to are growing away from us and they are unwilling or unable to include us or take us with them in the next chapter of their life. Regardless of whether they are unwilling or unable to include us, we feel like we are losing that friendship and if they leave, we are losing them.

If I change, I think it's because I'm growing. I expect you to understand my need to explore the world. But if you change, then I might experience it as betrayal because I am the one feeling left behind.

When anyone grows, it's a good thing. When we leave a friendship behind, it is a loss for both parties. Usually, it's just easier for the one that moves on to something new. The one left behind has a hole in their life that is not yet filled.

As friends, we need to be sensitive to any endings that come along and to help the other with that process. It is not against them, it is for us.

A great deal here depends on our attitude, and we get the life that goes with our attitude and perception. We're always more protective or kinder to our own change than we are of others'. When we are in a wonderful relationship and it begins to shift and the other person is unwilling or unable to include us, it hurts. There are times when it is easier for us if they are unable rather than unwilling, but either way, they are not in our lives. We are losing them. We are unable to be with them in the same way that we were.

In the best of situations, both of us are changing and we have to allow those changes. We can't expect that we are going to be exactly the same as we always have been. The work of friendship is staying connected and keeping in touch with people so we don't get out of sync. Learning to let go and to become less connected can lead to a different type of relationship, which hopefully fits for both persons.

Soul mates do not happen all the time. They are rare treasures. You can have a dear and wonderful loving friend and still not feel the person is a soul mate. My experience is with people who have stayed close for a lifetime. If you have a soul mate, you know it. It is part of risking a deep part of ourselves and knowing that that part of ourselves will be respected and cared for. If you don't have one, you have yet to have that experience.

ACTION ITEM ·········▶

Soul Searching

Do you have someone in your life with whom you share deeply, safely and confidently? Do they share your interests and values? Have you established a history of trust? Are you as concerned about their personal and spiritual growth as you are your own? Are they like a close brother or sister to you?

You can be married to someone and have a very good marriage with a very special person and still not be soul mates because that title belongs to another friend that you have.

Write about these connections in your journal.

Have you met and/or do you now have a soul mate? Call him or her and tell them thanks for being in your life.

Negotiating

At some point we negotiate—how much *me*, how much *we*. How much of the *self* am I willing to invest in this relationship? I may be willing to invest only about 80 percent—maybe you are willing to do 100 percent, but I only have 80 percent to give. So we negotiate back and forth. Everyone does this. Here's an example:

In the New Testament, Jesus is described as having a close and deep relationship with the apostles. The apostle Peter was particularly close to Jesus.

In a conversation between Jesus and Peter,

> Jesus said, "Peter, do you love (agape) me?"
> (Agape in Greek means unconditional, deep, spiritual love)
> Peter responds, "Yes Lord, you know I love (phileo) you."
> (The term phileo, in Greek, means brotherly or familial love.)
> Jesus again asks, "Peter, do you love (agape) me?"
> Peter answers again, "Yes, Lord, you know I love (phileo) you".
> Jesus asks one more time, "Do you love me"?
> (This time He uses the term phileo.)
> Peter responds, "Yes, Lord, you know I love you." (Uses the word phileo.)

Finally there is a match.

The reason I'm sharing this is that sometimes I get frustrated because I want a friend to love me or care about me as much as I love or care about them and they are unwilling or unable to do that. What I learned is that if Jesus cannot legislate the level of connection with another person, I certainly cannot! And neither can you.

It becomes a matter of negotiation. If someone says "*I* love you," and you respond, "I like you a lot too," we must notice the difference in language. At some point we realize we are negotiating with language. Perhaps here, we can say, it is Greek to me.

Negotiation always takes place around the issues of how much of the *self* is going to be invested in a relationship. That's what we do. It is an essential part of friendship.

If you want the richness of togetherness, negotiation is a part of the work. The layers and varieties of friendship include connections to help us feel less alone. A good day is a lot more fun and a bad day is bearable. Being a friend and having friends, from acquaintances to soul mates, leads to sharing, caring and a sense of community.

ACTION ITEM ·········▶

Mapping Your Relationships

Review your relationship maps and begin to notice who your intimate friends have been or are. Mark their circles with an F.

It's like when something really absurd happens to you and you don't realize how funny it is until you tell it to a friend. You both get such a kick out of it that it becomes an ongoing joke. You probably would have never thought about it again if you didn't share it with someone. Or when you're sitting at the dinner table with your boyfriend and family, and you and your mate look at each other at the same time, with the same look, and bust up laughing. You are thinking the same thing, you noticed the same thing. (Uma, 20)

> My best friend Emily and I are very connected. When we are together, we don't have to finish sentences, and can go from subject to subject staying with the conversation—AND knowing how one subject (totally unrelated to anyone else listening) flows from the previous one! My husband can't stay in the room with us when we're on a roll because he just can't keep up! The mutuality is endless, the resonance unstoppable. Even though we are 3,000 miles apart, when something happens to me, it's real when I can come home and call Emily to tell her. (Kathy, 30)

Your example of going to see Lily Tomlin really sank deep down. I have so much that I've done with my ex husband that I would love to do again with somebody else special to capture the fun, pleasure and smile out of it. To walk away and feel my experience was wonderful and complete. I, too, like you did, want to go back to "see it again." (Karen, 25)

> Julie showed up at my house and she brought me a beautiful rose from her garden. It smelled wonderful and it really helped to cheer me up. We spent the next few hours over coffee just talking and laughing, and I realized how lucky I am to have a friend like Julie who cares so much about me, that she would put aside all of her other plans just to be with me. (Brenda, 20)

I saw the movie M.A.S.H. in the early '70s in an Army theater in Europe, surrounded by a bunch of GIs and their wives.

Obviously, we mutually related to everything in the movie, and our resonance was hilarious. I've seen M.A.S.H. again since, and while it is still funny, the experience doesn't begin to compare. Needing someone to reinforce what we see as humor in a situation is the whole reason the laugh track was invented. (Naomi, 50)

> Bill was my best friend of all time, and I was his best friend. He and I were true soul mates. We shared our lives together. We didn't have to have any big plans to do anything, we just enjoyed being together. Sometimes we would double-date and go to the mountains or to the beach and enjoy each other's company. Other times we would just sit together somewhere, doing nothing in particular, and talk about anything and everything. He would say something and then I would add to it, or vice versa. Usually, we would wind up laughing so hard that tears would come to our eyes. (Bud, 60)

If I ever wondered why I love this class so much, it is the only place in my life, at this point, that I welcome both the process and the experience. I trust both, within the uterine safety of our classroom. I know I can both give and receive realness. The trust and affection, at least from my desk, is palpable. I want to listen to every word each person in the room says. I have grown so much through their experiences. I have grown so much by sharing my experiences with them. I have gained a new respect for many of the young women of the world; they have intelligence coupled with awareness that will take them to places my generation never envisioned. I had forgotten the joy of **we**. I had lost sight of the space between us and the joy of filling it with resonating voices—sharing, joining, and becoming more powerful than one voice alone. What a great experience this has been for a hermit. (Nica, 58)

> The phrases "yes, exactly" and "I know what you mean" have always been music to my ears. Being with someone who understands where I'm coming from is like slipping into a steaming Jacuzzi after a hard day's work. (Randy, 34)

Guy friends are the best because they are low maintenance. (Adam, 21)

Chapter 16

Love: A Few Comments

"For one human being to love another human being: that is perhaps the most difficult task that has been entrusted to us, the ultimate task. . ."

— Rainer Maria Rilke

What book on relationships would be complete without some comments on love? Perhaps we all need to think through our own personal definition of love.

You might ask when it comes to making a few comments on love, what can one say that hasn't already been said? In this chapter, I share thoughts on the fantasy of love, the fun of it, sometimes the fear of it and, lest we forget, the work of it. The bottom line may be that real love is a decision, one that requires fidelity and commitment.

Ruthellen Josselson said that people live with both their fantasies of love and their experiences of love. In addition to the difficulties and responsibilities of loving, let's take time to look at the fantasy and reality of our experiences. What kind of fantasies do you have and where did they begin?

Our love fantasies were fueled with childhood fairytales that always ended with *happily ever after*. Every soap opera, movie and love song we have been exposed to has fed those fantasies. Then we add our own wants and needs to the mix.

We hold out an ideal — something that we want and something semi-programmed into us about what *love is*. We study our families and our friends' families. We read poetry and watch movies. We listen to love songs and we have experiences that are so joyful we wish to repeat them. Also, we may have experiences as we grow that are not so good. Sometimes we have interactions with family members, friends, lovers and neighbors that do not follow the happily ever after script.

We may stay focused on the fantasy ideal and pretend that the reality experiences didn't happen or that they won't impact us. We are terribly surprised when they do impact us.

We have already discussed making a list of what a healthy relationship looks like and the qualities we are looking for, and we've decided that it's best for us to BE those qualities on the list first, *before* we choose to seek out someone who also has those desirable qualities.

Nevertheless, we search for love using a combination of those experiences, both positive and negative. We even add to the list, "I will never choose someone like so-and-so, ever." Or, "I will never be like or choose someone like my parents or siblings or first partner." We add a negative list to our positive wants, whether or not we write them down. It's our negative list that contributes to our fear of love and commitment. Our fear is that we won't be as happy as we want to be or that if we fall in love, we will be deeply hurt instead of deeply loved. So our search for love and the person we want to receive it from continues.

Love Recipe

Some people look to a simple recipe for love and relationships. If we follow that recipe, we are supposed to get the desired results. Yet we tend to be more complicated than a cookie recipe. We secretly slip in some *extra desired ingredients* without telling the other person what our fantasy expectations are.

Our fantasies include many things, but among them is that the other person will truly care about our needs and wants and do what they can to help us meet our needs. Their fantasy is that we will know and meet their needs as well.

Fantasies have ingredients. Sometimes fantasies have more ingredients and expectations than our realities. Perhaps this will make more sense if we look at the ingredients in a recipe. We all have the same needs (ingredients) but the amount of those needs changes depending on what we got or didn't get as we were growing up. I may need more holding than you do or have a greater desire for attachment. A big dose of trustworthiness may be at the top of my list for reasons you may not understand.

Most people would list the ingredients of chocolate chip cookies to include the following:

Chocolate Chip Cookie Recipe
2¼ cups flour
¾ cup brown sugar
¾ cup white sugar
1 cup nuts
2 eggs
1 bag chocolate chips
½ tsp salt
2 sticks butter
1 tsp baking soda
2 tsp vanilla

From these ingredients, we would expect, if we followed the recipe, to get some great homemade cookies.

What if the ingredients were not changed but the quantities were?

My "Unique" Chocolate Chip Cookie Recipe
¼ cup flour
4 cups brown sugar
1 tsp white sugar
4 nuts
1 dozen eggs
8 chocolate chips

1   cup salt
½   tsp butter
1   cup baking soda
1   qt vanilla

This is a unique recipe. With that quart of vanilla you would have to drink my cookies, you couldn't chew them. While the two recipes have the same ingredients, you noticed the quantities lead to very different results. You probably wouldn't choose my cookies over those made with the more traditional ingredient amounts.

The quality of a chocolate chip cookie changes when it is composed of different ingredients, or amounts. So, too, the quality of a relationship changes when an individual exhibits different personal needs and gifts to share—in different amounts—from our own. And, each other person has their list of ingredients or shopping list in their search for a special other as well.

As in every chapter of this book, it's important to remember that each of us has different quantities of needs which make up the ingredients in our list of fantasies, wants and desires as regards a mate or friend.

The ins and outs of our relationships are created by each of our unique recipes or expectations for love. Everyone reading this book has his or her own unique recipe or shopping list, which is different from everyone else's. Remember in Chapter 1, What Are Relationships For?, when we brainstormed what we wanted in a relationship? That information is directly related to this love recipe.

The quality of love changes when it is composed of different needs and desires. If we focus on a recipe of sex and fun as opposed to good potential for parenting and a supportive partner, we may get a completely different candidate. Being clear about our needs and desires will help us when shopping for a partner. Communicating clearly about our needs and desires will also help our partners to meet those needs.

Few of us will totally satisfy all the needs of another person, which is why we need a community of people involved in our lives. A community of people takes the pressure off of our significant other to meet all and every need we have. The community of our friends spreads the love and the fun and the variety of interests so that when we return to our partner/mate, we return refreshed and reenergized.

In other chapters, we discussed what other people contribute to us and which unique needs should be designated for our mate to meet. Our friends provide a loving environment while, hopefully, our mate provides intimate love.

This love recipe may also be confused by the merchandising of love in a materialistic society—that is, when love is promoted as a product or goods or something to trade, it's hard to know when we've gotten a good deal or our share. How much love are we entitled to? Do I have as much love as you do? How do you measure your love? Is it the size of the diamond engagement ring that determines how much you are loved? Perhaps in your relationship, you got a Mercedes, and your friend got a Volkswagen in theirs. Does this mean that you are loved more than your friend? Does this bring in the element of competition for external measures of love? It seems so.

That's the commodity part; relationships become merchandised and feed our fantasies. It becomes all about appearances.

How is your list of desired traits in your partner impacted by the advertisements in a bride's magazine or a men's magazine? Does the cost of a wedding have anything to do with the success of the relationship? Where in the advertisements does it refer to elements of relationships like respect, connecting, caring, nurturing, trusting, protecting and loving?

Merchandising and advertisements have nothing to do with the work of love or the heartfelt soul mate kinds of loving.

Becoming the *beautiful couple* is about the exterior appearance not the internal experience. Being preoccupied with material stuff, which ultimately will be replaced, will devalue the connection of human relationships.

The Look of Love

I think Scott Peck has created a wonderful discussion of love in his book *The Road Less Traveled*. I encourage you to take a look at his book. He discusses love as being concerned with the other person's spiritual growth. He also says it is a permanently self-enlarging experience. Certainly focusing on your partner's spiritual growth is more unselfish than measuring only "what's in it for me."

The Bible gives us a look at love when it says, "If I have all faith so as to move mountains but do not have love, I am nothing. Love is patient, love is kind. It is not jealous, [love] is not pompous, it is not inflated, it is not rude, it does not seek its own interests, it is not quick-tempered, and it does not brood over injury, it does not rejoice over wrongdoing but rejoices with the truth. . . . So faith, hope, love remain, these three; but the greatest of these is love."

When love is defined with a spiritual dimension, greater maturity is required. This definition of love challenges each of us to grow more, to be more concerned about others than ourselves, and by all means to support our loved ones without delivering careless hurtful words or actions. Can you relate to this?

The intense feeling level of love is familiar in our experiences of its beginnings, endings, or its absence. Sustaining that level during the relationship is yet another challenge. In the beginning of love, there is great excitement and a longing to be together physically and emotionally. In the endings of love, there is an anguish recalling the intensity of beginnings and all the good of the relationship. In the absence of love there is a heightened fantasy of all that could be and that is longed for.

The greatest challenge is to sustain the fun, playfulness, joy and delight of being with the other over time and to be careful not to take the other for granted.

One of my students, Carol Oh, wrote the following:

Love is the key to your boxed up feelings.
It makes you feel joy like you've never felt,
Pain that you think you can't endure,
Desires that have no reasoning or boundaries,
Fear of losing what is and should never be owned,
Gives you strength like you can move mountains
And opens your heart and mind to endless possibilities.

There is a practical need for choosing wisely those we love. There is a need for self-protection both physically and emotionally from feelings that we identify as love but which may be rampant hormones with no brainwaves in operation. The poet David Whyte in his poem "Sweet Darkness" concludes... "anything or anyone that does not bring you alive is too small for you." John Steinbeck offered, "If you are in love...that's about the best thing that can happen to anyone. Don't let anyone make it small or light to you.

There is a need to "keep one's head" when merchandising and external advertising overwhelm "our list" and lead us to choose poorly and pay dearly.

Oh, if only this were simpler. It could be simpler if we were computers.

Technical Installation of Love

Imagine if you will what would happen if we could actually download a program of love. I received the following in an e-mail. For all of us that spend time on the computer, the following install program may seem familiar. It includes references to some of the distractions for love, which I think are quite perceptive. If only it were this easy to install love.

LOVE

Customer: I'm not very technical, but I think I am ready to install now. What do I do first?

CS Rep: The first step is to open your HEART. Have you located your HEART, Ma'am?

Customer: Yes I have, but there are several programs running right now. Is it okay to install while they are running?

CS Rep: What programs are running, Ma'am?

Customer: Let me see...I have PASTHURT.EXE, LOW-ESTEEM.EXE, GRUDGE.EXE, and RESENTMENT.COM running right now.

CS Rep: No problem. LOVE will automatically erase PASTHURT.EXE from your current operating system. It may remain in your permanent memory, but it will no longer disrupt other programs.

LOVE will eventually overwrite LOWESTEEM.EXE with a module of its own called HIGHESTEEM.EXE. However, you have to completely turn off GRUDGE.EXE and RESENTMENT.COM.

Those programs prevent LOVE from being properly installed. Can you turn those off ma'am?

Customer: I don't know how to turn them off. Can you tell me how?

CS Rep: My pleasure. Go to your Start menu and invoke FORGIVENESS.EXE. Do this as many times as necessary until GRUDGE.EXE and RESENTMENT.COM have been completely erased.

Customer: Okay, I'm done. LOVE has started installing itself automatically. Is that normal?

CS Rep: Yes it is. You should receive a message that says

it will reinstall for the life of your HEART. Do you see that message?

Customer: Yes I do. Is it completely installed?

CS Rep: Yes, but remember that you have only the base program. You need to begin connecting to other HEARTS in order to get the upgrades.

Customer: Oops...I have an error message already. What should I do?

CS Rep: What does the message say?

Customer: It says "ERROR 412—PROGRAM NOT RUN ON INTERNAL COMPONENTS". What does that mean?

CS Rep: Don't worry, Ms., that's a common problem. It means that the LOVE program is set up to run on external HEARTS but has not yet been run on your HEART. It is one of those complicated programming things, but in non-technical terms it means you have to "LOVE" your own machine before it can "LOVE" others.

Customer: So what should I do?

CS Rep: Can you find the directory called "SELF-ACCEPTANCE"?

Customer: Yes, I have it.

CS Rep: Excellent, you are getting good at this.

Customer: Thank you.

CS Rep: You're welcome. Click on the following files and then copy them to the MYHEART directory: FORGIVESELF.DOC, SELFESTEEM.TXT, REALIZE-WORTH.TXT, and GOODNESS.DOC. The system will overwrite any conflicting files and begin patching any faulty programming. Also, you need to delete

SELFCRITIC.EXE from all directories, and then empty your recycle bin afterwards to make sure it is completely gone and never comes back.

Customer: Got it. Hey! My HEART is filling up with really neat files. SMILE.MPG is playing on my monitor right now and it shows that WARMTH.COM, PEACE. EXE, and CONTENTMENT.COM are copying themselves all over my HEART!

CS Rep: Then LOVE is installed and running. You should be able to handle it from here. One more thing before I go...

Customer: Yes?

CS Rep: LOVE is freeware. Be sure to give it and its various modules to everybody you meet. They will in turn share it with other people and they will return some really neat modules back to you.

Customer: I will. Thank you for your help.

E-mail, source unknown

The Decision

Love is a gift and a decision, no matter where we find it. We learn from each experience. If we sat with friends and tried to agree on a definition of love, I believe we would find it to be a difficult and illusive task. We're different. We learn from our experiences. We learn from love and we learn from what we think is love and what may actually be a reaction to other needs.

You may have dated someone over a period of time even knowing that they were not the right one. You did it for reasons that made sense to you at the time. There may come a time, however, when you choose someone and with the decision comes the awareness that with this person, you will stay, no matter what.

Richard Bolles, author of *What Color Is Your Parachute?* wrote, "The model of all life is to act and then take time to reflect on it. The issue is never success or failure, but it is, what did you learn?" With each love experience, we grow when we ask ourselves, What did I learn from this?

Many times reviewing and replaying difficult relationships seems only to restimulate the pain. Revisiting the difficult relationships in order to pry loose learnings will allow us to truly leave the pain behind while taking the insights with us into new relationships. Perhaps we learn the most from tough times when they teach us something about ourselves.

Sometimes our "chooser" is broken and we pick poorly because we have not learned from our poor choices.

Perhaps looking at our attractions—those we are attracted to—through the filter of our shopping list will help us to choose better rather than choosing to repeat the same behavior with similar people to see if we can force it to turn out differently.

It may be that you have had a relationship where love was confused with control. "Love is not about power; in real love you want the other person's good. In romantic love, you want the other person," says Margaret Anderson. Here, romantic love seems to be related to ownership of another rather than sharing. There is a difference.

ACTION ITEM··········▶

Power Play

Who do you know that is into power and control in their relationships? How do you deal with that? Are you the power and control partner? What would happen if you gave up that control and just trusted your partner? Are they trustworthy? What power and control items were on your shopping list back in Chapter 11 on partner shopping?

Review your list. Write in your journal some of the thoughts that come to your mind.

The psychologist/philosopher Carl Jung wrote, "Where love reigns, there is no will to power: and where power predominates, there, love is lacking. The one is the shadow of the other." There is a separation. We can be clear about the fact that an abusive relationship is not about love.

More recently, Gloria Steinem added her observation: "There are many more people trying to *meet* the right person than who try to *become* the right person.

The man who falls in love with a strong and independent woman and then tries to tame her is not loving, but conquering.

The woman who is obsessed by the question, how can I change him? is not centered in her own life, but rather is trying to control his—a plot that is common when women "marry" their lives instead of "leading" them. You don't marry for a life; you have a life first, and then you marry."

If You Loved Me . . .

Have you ever caught yourself telling a mate or friend or lover or siblings or colleagues, "If you loved me, you would know what I want?" Perhaps this is disguised in something like, "If you loved me, you would know that on the third Friday of every month, I want you to surprise me with flowers." What is your favorite manipulative sentence? If you loved me, you would (fill in the blank here!). Do you say to your friends or partner, "You should just know that, if you loved me or really cared about me?"

Well, guess what? They don't know—because they are not mind readers. When statements are delivered like that, it becomes a signed, sealed and closed issue. The other person has no voice or opportunity to answer in this situation because you have become judge and jury and delivered the verdict about someone else's behavior and motives. Could you possibly be wrong?

We want other people to be mind readers. It would be nice if they were. We want them to be so attuned to us that they would sense without reminders exactly our needs or tastes at any given moment, but particularly on special anniversaries, birthdays, stress days, etc. We want their priorities to match ours. Are we mind readers where they are concerned? Probably we fall short in that category, too, but they, after all, should know.

We challenge them with their shortcomings and startle them with our accusations. When they look at us stunned as if to say, how would I know that, we are fully disgusted and believe that we have a good reason to go off in a snit! In fact, we have been so self-focused that we hardly noticed that they too had a point of view or priority. We might ask ourselves if our approach was a loving one. We might also revisit the Biblical guidelines for loving, which call for us to choose our own response to and interpretation of the other person's behavior and keep in mind their needs.

I think the expectations that lead to the previous issue speak to the work of relationships. The work is staying in tune with the other and not jumping to conclusions of familiarity. Finishing sentences for each other does not mean that we do so correctly.

Assigning meaning to someone's behavior without checking it out with them can also be in error, even when it comes from a loving intimate place. Keeping love in tune requires daily attention. The work of love also requires including the fun of love on a regular basis as an antidote to the problems of a love relationship.

This is a short chapter on a huge topic. There is no attempt here to cover all the ins and outs of love. We have looked briefly at fantasies, recipes, guidelines and power issues. The spiritual view can set the tone. The problems do challenge us. There is so much to think about. These few highlights may bring some thoughts to you to wrap around the other chapters that speak to deep and trusting relationships.

Ultimately, love is about a decision or a series of them. Dr. Martin Luther King, Jr. agrees, when he states, "Love requires character. It is a decision."

After the attraction, courtship, togetherness, dreams, fantasies, excitement, plateaus and problems, choosing another person to spend your life with is about a moment of decision to love, followed by a decision for fidelity and then a decision of commitment. You have chosen to stay.

Love is wonderful, love is work, love grows, and love ultimately requires a decision. Choose wisely.

ACTION ITEM ··········➤

Mapping Your Relationships

As you review your relationship maps, mark an L or draw a heart in the circles of those that you have chosen to love and those you believe have chosen to love you.

Can you identify moments when you chose to love someone? What do you think brought you to that moment? Write down a few thoughts in your journal.

I love feeling prized and cherished and being a priority to someone. Never did I feel like that before, never was I this secure and free at the same time. Sometimes I even think that nothing else matters in the world, just us. (Irene, 34)

> It is an awesome feeling to be in love. It can't be described, only experienced. (Brent, 36)

Mitch is part of me, and I am part of him. We have created a union, yet we are also separate individuals. We have a relationship that is strong enough to acknowledge the space between us. We accept each other's strengths and weaknesses, communicate honestly, have respect for each other and support each other's personal growth. When I think of the word 'passion', all of these elements come to mind. Passion encompasses more than just physical drive. It also includes empathy, respect, attachment and validation. If Mitch and I had a marriage based on physical passion only, we would be heading to marriage counseling. (Lenore, 27)

> All in all the most important of all these things is how we love, love our God first, and how we love our brothers, and how we love our selves. (Josh, 39)

Love is the passion of one lover for another, the mutuality of shared experience, the gratitude for understanding and validation, the security of being adequately held. (Ona, 25)

"I love you, not only for who you are, but who I am when I am with you."

—Elizabeth Browning

Will you marry me and be my mommy?

Chapter 17

Tending Is Not for the Timid

*"Everybody can be great, because anybody can serve. You
don't have to have a college degree to serve. You don't
have to make your subject and verb agree to serve. You
only need a heart full of grace. A soul generated
by love."*

— Martin Luther King, Jr.

*Perhaps the most challenging task of our lives is the
tending of others. It requires the best of us and demands
unbelievable energy. Sculpting the care to meet
the custom needs of the person in a way acceptable
to them requires insight, struggle and strategy.*

At no time during relationships is the demand for love
greater than when tending of the other is required.

There are levels of care giving. Some require that we offer
our attention and listening. Some require that we reach into
the very fiber of our being to care for loved ones that are suffering greatly. Tending someone contributes to bonding with
that person. Even professional caregivers report bonding with
their patients.

A newborn baby gets round-the-clock loving care and
thrives. The baby's parents are sleep deprived, exhausted, and
can barely think because of the demands of care giving.

A hospitalized friend rests with professional care while her parents, friends and/or partner drive daily, visit during appropriate hours and become fatigued with the physical and emotional demands of caring.

An aging parent requires extra care either in their home or in a senior citizen home or assisted living facility. The tending adult child works full-time and cares full-time, paying bills, looking after medications, interfacing with doctors, and trying to provide quality time visits. The double life takes its toll. There are not enough hours in the day.

Have you been the caregiver for a child and/or an elderly person? Think back to that time and what it felt like, what it meant to you, and what it still means to you. Chances are the memories are a combination of tender loving feelings and inner anguish or turmoil or perhaps physical exhaustion. Maybe you have not yet experienced these demands and have no clue of what is ahead. This chapter refers to some key areas related to tending.

Children, while incredibly demanding, will eventually grow into self-sufficiency while the aging experience the losses leading to the end of their life. Children are growing up, moving ahead, and learning something new, and our hope as we care for them is that they will be able to take care of themselves at a certain point.

Although the aging adult can often verbalize what their difficulties are as compared with the wordless infant, they also have to deal with their own feelings as they face their losses. Some anger is involved, and if you happen to be the closest target, you may be the one to catch it. Custom tailoring the tending becomes a challenge.

When we are tending, we offer to others the best of ourselves. We may offer our money or time, but REAL tending occurs out of our emotional resources, from our deep internal feelings. In contrast, if we do not have a strong center ourselves, we cannot truly tend. We do not tend in a way that the other person can respond to because instead of deep caring, we are tending in a distant, shallow, superficial way. Our children, our friends, our family can sense the difference between genuine caring and superficial mechanical motions.

If someone is caring for us, we feel their genuine concern, or its absence. This is best illustrated by being tended by someone who doesn't care.

Whether it's a haircut, the doctor or a customer service desk, we can tell if someone wants to help us, or if they "frankly don't give a damn." The same thing is true with someone who waits on us in a store. Sometimes they are so busy doing something else that you have to work at getting their attention just to pay for your purchase. They don't give you the time of day.

We sense when someone doesn't care, and we also can sense when someone does. It is a strong message, and while we may not know how to put it into words, we certainly do know the difference.

ACTION ITEM··········➤

Tender Feelings

Recall a time when you were well tended or not tended at all? How did you feel? What worked for you? What if anything hurt you?

We need tending all of our lives—from each other, our families, our mates/partners and in our workplace. While we are paid to perform our duties, we still benefit when support from our colleagues is present. We all need support in the different arenas of our lives.

There is also the daily tending we give back to our partners or mates and family members as well as friends. This requires taking time to listen, share, support, enjoy and respond from our best self.

We provide simple tending out of love when we:

- Go to the grocery store for someone
- Drop them off in front of the theater while we go park the car
- Do the dusting or cleaning when company is coming
- Help with the dishes after a dinner party
- Pick up the check at a restaurant
- Take a casserole over to a sick friend
- Drive a neighbor to a doctor's appointment
- Pick up someone's kids after school or a school event

Tending is more demanding when we:

- Sit beside someone who is in the hospital
- Spend time with someone who is terminally ill
- Support a spouse or children when a family member has died
- Listen to a friend who is going through a break up
- Participate in a therapy group when someone you love needs you to be there

Mother Teresa described it as being a little pencil in the hand of a writing God who is sending a love letter to the world.

Tending Is Powerful

The circle of life requires that we take turns. Isn't it interesting that we start out our lives being held and later when we have matured, we are counted on to hold others? The root word of tend (a shortened form of 'attend') is ten (tenere) which is Latin, for "to hold" (pay attention to or to look after).

When we decide to care for others, we make a strong statement and a declaration of what we stand for in our lives. These everyday decisions determine our priorities. Albert Schweitzer taught that "the only ones among you who will be really happy are those who will have sought and found how to serve." This is quite a challenge.

The Worth of Tending

Tending is not a moneymaker. Think for a minute, whom do we pay more, the people who tend children or the people who tend money? The answer is: The people who tend money of course. What does that say about our priorities?

If I had a stack of money, it wouldn't go anywhere, it wouldn't stick its finger in a light bulb socket or run across the street somewhere. It just sits there. However, I would be paid more to look after that money than I would to look after a child who is at risk in a daily life situation, and who could take off in two seconds in all different directions. While money, investments, earnings, etc. do need tending, our children are our country's number one resource for the future. So, what's wrong with this unbalanced picture?

The value our culture places on caretaking is really off center. I wonder what would happen if, in our culture, real success was measured by having healthy relationships. Our whole culture would have a different look. If we said families and interpersonal relationships were a higher priority, our school curriculum would be different, our families would be different and our country would be different.

Schools would include classes on human relationships. Parents would spend more time at home with each other and with their children than at the office. Our country would invest more money in health care, literacy and family education and neighborhood recreation and safety. Families would be stronger. Fewer dollars would be necessary for gang intervention and drug enforcement. We give lip service to the importance of our interpersonal relationships, but we do not put our tending energies there.

Prioritize

What do you stand for, and where do you put your priorities and energy? Write some of these things down in your journal.

Tending Does Not Come Easily

When you have a child you do the best you can to tend them. You try different things and when some of them work you're thrilled. You try other things and some of them don't work, but eventually you figure out what works with this child.

A second child may come along and you'll try the same things that worked with child number one, and they don't work at all. You ask yourself what's wrong with the story here; how come it doesn't work? So you have to think of something else. You work really hard at figuring out what will work with child number two.

Then your third child comes along and you try what worked with children one and/or two. It doesn't work so you have to try something new once again. What works with one person is ineffective for another. Tending is a custom tailored, continually rethinking task!

When women go through menopause, sometimes everyone around them is subject to her mood swings and emotional outbursts. Being low on estrogen can require that others have remarkable patience. The task of tending to her (and living with her) is one of tolerance as well as gentleness.

When a partner or friend is going through a difficult time at work, listening to them and helping them figure out a strategy to overcome their difficulty takes time. Sometimes when you're trying to help someone, they'll say, "You're not doing it right — this is not helping me."

So when we talk about the process of tending and giving

care, we are talking about a process that develops through patience and reflection. We try something and then we see if it worked, or if there is something better we could do.

A caring partner I know says to his wife every day, "What can I do to make your life better today?" How would you like to hear that daily?

Listening, valuing and showing respect are keys to caring for others and for showing them you do care.

Surviving the Caring

In order to balance and meet their needs, you have to come up with a strategy, and then in order to take care of yourself as well, you have to do more thinking and strategizing.

Consider what the airline flight attendants say when giving onboard safety briefings. "Put on your own oxygen mask first and then adjust your child's mask"—not the other way around. Why not? If you cannot help yourself, you cannot help your child. If in fumbling to help your child you do not get enough oxygen and can't breathe—which happens very quickly—then you are both lost. If you take care of yourself first, then you are in a position to help others.

I've shared this analogy frequently with parents of teenagers who are exhausted by trying to keep up with their teen's moods. "Adjust your own facemask first," I say. Take care of yourself, too, by having some fun along the way.

You have to remember to take time out for yourself, because if you don't, you are going to run out of gas. You and the "tendee" are both going to have problems.

It takes hard work, reflection, thinking and strategy.

Lack of Tending

Maybe there was a time when you were helplessly untended, and if that's the case, you had to develop some defenses against your need for care and letting others tend to you.

I had some contact with a woman colleague who, it seemed

to me, didn't have much trust. She was defensive and often accusing. She would say, "What do you mean by that? You can't count on that." She was always negative. One day I said, "I don't understand, why is it that you just cannot trust people?" She spun around and yelled at me, "Because when I was a child I was left in the car in the dark alone while my parents were in the bar. When they came out, they were always drunk and I never knew what was going to happen. I was scared to death in that car, alone, in the parking lot, in the dark."

In that moment, an adult who had raised two children became a six-year-old child again. She had the terrifying experience of being helplessly untended. She distrusted people to be there for her and was defensive. That came directly from the experience of feeling left alone and untended.

A teen student of mine went home each day to check on her terminally ill father. Every time she entered the home, she wondered if he was still alive. This daily burden took its toll on her, and by the end of the school year she was emotionally shut down.

When we're not able to express care, and someone needs it and we just don't have the resources to give, we can feel empty inside. There is something inside of us that withers when we don't extend care to someone who is in need. To be indifferent to the needs of others is to be cold. To hold others with so little value is not to value one's self.

Parenting

I'm working with a pregnant teenager who thinks that you have a baby and then live happily ever after. She has no sense or understanding about what is required to provide 24/7 care of an infant. Seemingly, it's impossible to get that information to her at this time before she personally experiences it. She has to find out for herself if she can meet that demand. It requires unselfishness, focus and an attitude of tending.

We usually think of someone who is tending as someone who is raising a child. It goes beyond that, in that when we take care of someone, we take on the problems or the worries that they have.

You know of course that kids don't care how much you know until they know how much you care. All those we tend want to know if we care.

The Conflict of Tending

There is a close relationship between love and hate. How can that be? As a mother, you care very deeply for your child, but there are times when you resent your child. "I love my child, I'm devoted to my child, but gee, I wish I had a life. If it wasn't for this child, I could go out tonight with my friends; I could be free to play and do something else, but instead I'm stuck here with you — oh, lovely child."

In those moments, tending is full of conflict. Going to the hospital daily to see someone can wear us out, particularly if it is a long-term care situation. We do it because we love them, they need us, and we care for them, but we become exhausted. There is a moment when love and hate can be right there together; I hate being here, and I love you — and now I feel guilty for even saying that out loud. The hatred is made up of the frustration, resentment and helplessness that you feel.

So, we turn it inward; how can I love my child and resent him at the same time? I must be a bad person. Tending brings all these feelings of guilt, resentment and love together. The problem is that tending is hard work. It is not the work for the timid. You are making a commitment and doing the hardest part of a relationship because you are giving from a special place in yourself and setting yourself aside for the moment or many moments. You are saying, I am making you a priority — I am giving to you from my heart.

When discussing care we realize that love and hate are

closely connected and not opposite from each other. Love and hate are very close to each other; they are both very intense. Usually we think, "Well, I either love you or I hate you." Actually, hate is not the opposite of love. Indifference is! The line from *Gone with the Wind*, when Rhett says to Scarlet, "Frankly, my dear, I don't give a damn," really says it all.

The Endings of Tending

If we are going through a relationship break up and we say to someone, "I hate you" — we are investing tremendous emotional energy towards that person. It may take more investment of energy to hate than it does to love them. The reason we hate them at that moment is because we used to love them, or we hate them because they used to love us and now they don't. We miss their attention and their tending.

We may be fighting over money, who gets custody of the refrigerator, how are we going to divide up the photo albums, etc. All of that stuff centers around love and hate; they are quite close together.

If you really want to know if you are over someone, check your own temperature. If you are fairly indifferent to them, you have probably moved on, but if you still hate them, your energy is still very much wrapped up with them.

Anger and Tending

Dr. Elizabeth Kubler Ross pointed out that "as human beings we become angry, which is normal, healthy and natural, as long as it does not last more than forty-five seconds. You can flare-up and burn brightly for forty-five seconds. If it lasts longer, then it's not about what is happening, it is about your baggage.

When we beat ourselves up for more than forty-five seconds, we are arguing history and all the previous times we have made the same dumb mistake.

To get rid of it you must recognize your anger and then you

can do something about it. It is when you are not aware of it that it sneaks up on you. Extract information from your anger and learn from it, rather than keeping it alive.

When we have personal baggage and we haven't done anything with it, it stays with us.

Bury Your Anger, Literally!

As you work through your anger areas, instead of keeping them on your mind, write them down on a piece of paper, put it in a box and then go dig a hole in your backyard and bury that box as deep as you can. If at any time you think you are going to forget all the things you are/were angry about or that were bothering you, go back, dig it up and go through the pages. Otherwise, leave it buried.

Why is anger in the tending chapter?

Emotions are complicated and with the elderly, they are even more complicated for us and for them. They may have anger surrounding their illness.

We have anger at the illness that is taking the person away from us. We have anger at the energy drain and we are sometimes at war with ourselves for a variety of things.

How do we maintain boundaries in a crisis? We must care for the other and anticipate their needs. We must manage what needs to be managed and communicate with other family members about what is happening.

Be sensitive to yourself here. You may have memories to deal with that bring up old resentments with the grieving. Many times the person being cared for isn't always a pleasant soul to deal with.

You may have good memories to deal with and the remembered good times might also make you sad. Yes, tending involves grieving.

265

Be sensitive to your own needs. Remember to tend to your own oxygen mask during this process. Take time for yourself.

Taking Turns

Think about a time when you needed attention or tending and you went to a friend. Perhaps you went up to someone and said you are really having a difficult day and wanted to share it with them, and the next thing you know, they launch into "I know what you mean … me too! It was just awful. Let me tell you about it…" After which they go on for thirty-five minutes about their problems. How does that make you feel? You want to be tended by someone and instead they take advantage of your subject matter and dump their load back on you. Do they think they are being helpful? Probably. Are they? Probably not.

The rule here is that if you are going to be successful at tending others, you have to be able to put aside your own experience — at least briefly. Count to at least ten before you jump in and say you know what they mean and you've gone through it too. If you have to, take your hand and put it over your mouth! Make that ten count, and then say, "Would you like to talk about it?" Then put your hand back over your mouth so you won't get in the way of yourself tending. Remember that sometimes the toughest thing in the world to do is to sit quietly and listen.

Some time ago a friend of mine's son died. I was staying with her for the weekend and we were talking late into the night. I was trying to tend her, and at one point she was talking about how she was feeling, the tragedy of it all, and I said "I know how you feel." The next thing I knew, she just angrily yelled at me saying "You don't know how I feel, you haven't been through it!"

She was right, I didn't know how she felt and I used those words because I was trying to be with her, but they were the wrong words. I now say, "It must be awful." Then I just listen. Even if I had had a similar experience, I still wouldn't know how she felt at that moment in time.

The problem with tending someone else is to know *how* to be with that person — not offend them, or set them off — but just to simply be with them. It takes thinking about it to come up with a strategy... and discipline to oftentimes hold your tongue. Tending is sometimes just being there.

I think sometimes we do a dis-service by not allowing a person to be where they are. This is particularly so when you are coping with a person who has a terminal illness. They have some work to do as they let go of their lives. They may go to a very different place emotionally than you think they are going to go, but they are doing what they need to do. Part of that may be allowing the person to say to you, "Yes, I'm dying and I want to talk to you about that." If you give them the opportunity, it may pay off. Decide whose needs you are tending.

Think about this: How many times has someone helped you and for the next year or so they went around telling everyone how much they did for you? They take credit for how much they helped you when you were greatly in need; they tell your story at every party, etc. This feels terrible. Aren't you sorry you accepted their help?

When we are helpful to someone else, we have to remember whose needs we are serving. When we focus on their needs, we do not expect credit or thanks for what we are doing. It is simply our gift to them.

If we tend good enough we have a sense of warmth, sharing, caring and giving. If we cannot rise to the occasion, we have a sense of indifference to other people's needs. If we overdo the tending of others, we are not taking care of ourselves and we become compulsive caregivers... not a good thing. It's a matter of balancing our needs and theirs.

The Dalai Lama put it simply, "If you want others to be

Tending Is Not for the Timid

happy, practice compassion. If you want to be happy, practice compassion."

By attending to others' needs, we share ourselves. We contribute as a giver and as a receiver and have created an opportunity to bond. Bonding is a part of togetherness that works and the art and work of tending strengthens relationships.

ACTION ITEM ··········▶

Mapping Your Relationships

Review your relationship maps and find the people who tended you and mark their circles with RT (received tending) and GT (gave tending) in the circles of those you tended.

So starts my lifelong quest to secretly be Mother Theresa, Florence Nightingale, and the Singing Nun rolled into one! (Kathy, 30)

> I didn't have a mother to tend me and it would have been nice to have someone to bake cookies for me and listen to my boy stories. Then I realized I have one of those, but his name is Daddy, and he is the best because he proves every day that he is more than I could ever ask for in a parent. (Dee, 20)

I don't view myself as a particularly nurturing or caring person. Frankly, I was raised to just survive and learned nothing of truly tending to the needs of others. My hope is that with time and prayer I will mature and give, intend, attend and extend myself much more than I do now. My husband is a very loving and caring person. The more time I spend with him, the better I feel about tending and care giving. Perhaps it's because I'm getting some of my own emotional needs met, which is in turn expanding my capacity to love. (Fiona, 30)

> For the rest of my life, I will always remember that I am only allowed to be angry for forty-five seconds; this has been a large problem in my life. I am an angry person, so I tend to hold grudges and only look at one side of the story. (Rachel, 31)

My mother is the classic example of tending to the point of martyrism. She isn't happy unless she's miserable. (Naomi, 50)

> To tend and be tended makes me feel my little existence matters somehow. My life is enriched every time I extend myself to console or validate a child or friend. Continued mutual tending fills up my soul. (Mary Lou, 45)

I find joy in helping and comforting those in need. I love tending to my husband and children. For me tending is a balancing act. If I feel taken advantage of or taken for granted, resentfulness can creep in. That's when I step back and do something for myself. I have learned to accept care from others more comfortably than I used to. It has always been easier for me to give than to receive. (Ona, 34)

> I feel that I spend most of my time tending my children. I find that I seldom get a break and it's very overwhelming at times. I've posted the statement "Adjust your own face mask first" next to my bed, as a reminder to take care of myself first. I learned that it is normal sometimes to feel resentful or overwhelmed when tending someone else, even if you love them very much. (Odile, 46)

I thought it was really neat, how, even though humans are a very selfish species, always trying to get things from others, that what we fear is that we may lack the ability to give. That really made me think. I also liked the part about love and hate being "parallel but opposite streams of experience." That is so incredibly true. (Sandi, 20)

Now I realize that I am not the caring person that I thought I was. I do a lot of things in order to receive what I need. So much of my actions are based on me and there is a lot of self-centeredness in my perspective. I have become pretty damn good at manipulating myself to believe that I am a caring and giving person when I don't know the first thing about it. I do for others so that I can have from them what I need. (Dee, 20)

In addition to tending and caring for my three young children, I provided care to my father during the last three years of his life before he died of cancer. Somehow, my bond with him was so strong that it never felt in any way like a burden to me. However, I am presently feeling guilty about the fact that I do not really want to take on the responsibility of being my mother's caregiver. I am caught between a sense of responsibility towards her and the knowledge that my marital situation is so fragile that I cannot tend to so many people without having a single person tending to me! (Bee, 31)

I realize now how hard it is to care for someone so deeply and to tend to a person as well. It also scares me a bit, too, because I'm an only child, which means that the responsibility to care for both of my parents when they get older is mine. (Winter, 22)

I cared for my mom when she had several broken vertebrae and I did so willingly and out of love for her. I believe my mom got frustrated occasionally because our roles were reversed with me taking care of her. I think she sometimes took out her frustrations on me. Then I felt resentment because of her response to my tending and then I felt guilt because of my resentment. (Diana, 34)

I am just so sick of being attached to people that I hold, who don't hold me. It is not fair. (Brenda, 19)

There are times when I think of myself as self-absorbed and uncaring because I can't find the energy to extend myself in this realm. Feelings of guilt then saturate my mind and I tend in a way that doesn't feel like it's truly from my heart. This, of course, leaves me feeling empty and despondent. I want the recipient to understand that it's not that I don't care; I just may not be up to providing what is required at that moment. I would rather not extend myself at all if it is not genuine and whole. I expect the same from others who care for me. There is nothing worse than receiving care from someone who is not emotionally involved in your situation. (Marnie, 23)

> Everyone needs tending to and everyone needs to tend. Your life cannot simply revolve around others because you may become bitter or forget your own needs, but your life definitely cannot revolve around your own self because you will never be satisfied within your own trap of selfishness. (Kara, 21)

Tending is Not for the Timid

It seems to me with all of the
languages on this earth we could find
one we both understand!!!

Oh, what in the world are
you talking about now?!!

Chapter 18

Gender Differences

*"Sometimes I wonder if men and women really suit each
other. Perhaps they should live next door and just visit
now and then."*

— Katharine Hepburn

**You've heard that men are from Mars and women are
from Venus, right? Henry Higgins in My Fair Lady
asked, why can't a woman be more like a man? Well,
men and women really are different! Understanding
those differences can lead to a reduction in frustration
on both our parts. Why can't men be more like women
and women more like men? Read (or listen) closely.**

If we could put our ears to the closed doorway of a little girl's
room while she's inside playing alone, what would we hear?
Most likely, we'd hear the conversations that she is having with
her dolls, stuffed animals and everything else in the room. She
uses different voices for her inanimate friends and she's dreaming up intricate stories about relationships, problems that they
are working out, shopping excursions and other creative ventures. They are discussing issues, and she is scolding the bad
toys. She is praising others and punishing some of them and
teaching them all lessons. She has an entire soap opera going
on inside that room. And it's all talking. It's all about relationships. "I don't understand, Teddy, why you can't get along with
Kitty; you're both very nice people and you both need to work
on your problems!"

In contrast, let's put our ear to the doorway of a little boy's room. What do you hear? He is exploding things, pounding, blowing up things, charging, making lots of noise, racing, competing, zooming. All this noise, things colliding—he is *doing* and it's exciting.

If you have raised both a boy and a girl, you learned quickly that they are different.

I was at a fast food restaurant recently, sitting behind a mother and two children. The mother had her back to me and in front of her were her little girl and boy. The little girl was having a conversation with her mother. The little boy was doing the most interesting things with French fries and ketchup that I've ever seen. He had them as close to the edge of the table as he could get them without them falling off. He made sound effects and bumped the fries into each other. The ketchup provided the "color" for the attacks!

Although not very appetizing to me, he was having a great time. His sister's conversation had nothing to do with him—he was busy *doing* and she was simply *being*. He was physically active—she was communicating. Men *do*—women *be*. Perhaps that is the stereotypic difference between the two genders! In fact, in Yoga, "being" is practiced and encouraged no matter what the gender.

As we age, women continue to talk when they get together. Women continue to treat relationships as a priority in their lives. Men continue to share an activity and do things together, like building something or going fishing or attending a sports event or playing basketball. They tend to focus on their careers. Gloria Steinem commented, "I have yet to hear a man ask for advice on how to combine marriage and a career."

I've heard some other differences described like this:

- Men talk to negotiate and women talk to bond.
- Men tend to use substances (eat, drink or use drugs) not to know what they feel.

- Women tend to use substances (eat, drink or use drugs) not to feel what they know.
- Men want to be respected and women want to be cherished.
- Men have been raised not to show their feelings (although that is changing in some families) and women have been taught to be charming so that men will be attracted to them.

Women's lib has focused on breaking barriers to allow women the same opportunities as men have. Some men, in response, are sensing loss of control of traditional roles and do not know what to do about their feelings. Other men enjoy the liberation of sharing those roles.

No matter what else, men and women develop different-ly, physically and mentally. Their brains function differently. Males tend to favor either left or right brain dominance while females tend to be more whole brained. Left brained activities are math and science, using logic and sequential thinking and lots of structure. Right brained activities include music and art and movement. It is the creative side of our brain and is spontaneous and intuitive.

Women can go back and forth from left to right brained more easily while men tend to stay on one side or the other.

Men traditionally have greater upper body strength. Women have better fine motor co-ordination and much lower incidence of color blindness.

Societal expectations for men and women are different and still put pressure on each gender to behave according to certain norms, no matter how far we have come in accepting our respective uniqueness.

And no matter how we try to homogenize the genders, male and female behavior is different. Just take a look at the behavior of young boys and girls to verify that.

We are different.

Sex?

Leonard Shlain writes "boys think with their penises, girls think with their hearts. Neither gender thinks with their brains."

Young people ask many questions about sex. The time differences to sexual satisfaction are not always understood. Essentially, for young men, from zero to blast off is about sixty seconds. For young women to be satisfied, it usually takes much longer. He would ask, "How come she is so slow?" She would ask, "Why is he in such a hurry?"

He can't help it—that's the way he's designed. She can't help it, that's the way she is designed. It is necessary to understand that difference if you want to pleasure your partner. You have to know that there is a difference in timing.

Sharing with each other sexually, beyond just the sex act, requires communication and sensitivity to your partner's needs. Communication requires maturity, which is a step ahead of adolescence. This is why it is a good idea for teenagers to wait until they are older to have sexual intercourse. There are also the issues of readiness, personal values and religious beliefs.

Adolescence and Sexuality

One of the things that will begin to make some sense for us is if we begin to look at development in adolescence. In adolescence we fully feel "everything." We feel all of our emotions. Because of our blooming hormones, it's a wonderful time and a terrible time. But this, and pre-adolescence, is the time when we are actively learning about sexuality.

This is a time when the stakes get higher. There are demands from peers to "fit in", from the school to "perform", from parents to "behave", and from extended family to make them proud. In most cultures, gender demands and expectations do not allow much wiggle room as to how an adolescent is to express his or her gender identity.

Boys will be boys. Girls will be girls. By junior high, demands from the peer group bully, enforce, mediate and model a strict code of gender specific behavior. The girl is required to dress according to the peer group standard or be teased or excluded from the "in" group. If the boy looks different, or acts different from the main group, he may receive hurtful remarks referring to his sexual preference. Thou shalt conform or pay a terrible price.

Defining Adolescence

I enjoyed hearing the following definition of adolescence when I was attending a parenting workshop.

> Put the personality of a child in the body of an adult, furnish a need to be loved and a fierce desire to be independent, allow a need to be self-directing but leave out any idea of what direction to take, add an enormous amount of love but also the fear that it may not be accepted or returned, give physical and sexual powers without any knowledge or experience of how to use them—and then, take these and place them in a society whose values and achievements are essentially incomprehensible and certainly unattainable and whose concerns are seemingly misplaced and insincere. Do this, and you have just begun to understand the problems of adolescence.

Do this, and you have also just begun to understand the problems of parents of adolescents.

For more about gender differences, check Chapter 10, Relating Sexually. Let's look at some other differences and see if we can understand that "other gender" more.

ACTION ITEM ··········▶

Gender Switch

Relax for a moment.

Take some slow deep breaths and then read each part that follows and take time to really go back and remember. Go slowly. Read slowly. Take your time.

After you read each line, you might want to close your eyes in order to go back to that time and place, to capture what it was like.

- Think back to some of your experiences in high school with the opposite sex.
- Think about whom you were attracted to.
- As you reflect, jot down some notes.
- Remember the group that you spent time with.
- Visualize what you wore, and what activities you enjoyed.
- Go back a little further to junior high or middle school. What did you like to do for fun?
- What about elementary school? What things did you like to do when you were playing?
- Can you remember any earlier memories of just being a kid?
- What was your status or place in your family?
- What was it like to be an infant in your family?

Picture the special day of your birth and your welcome into the family.

Now I want to wave my magic wand and announce that you have just been born — and you have been born a member of the other sex!

After the surprise, think about what might be different for you now that you are the other gender. Imagine! Would you be more or less comfortable being the other gender?

Picture what would have been different for you as a child in terms of your playtime, in your family, and in your neighborhood.

- When you go to elementary school, what is different?

- In junior high, do the stakes get higher?
- What does it feel like to be in high school as a member of the other gender? How different would that experience have been for you?
- Who would your friends be?
- What is it like to date?
- If you were a boy, would you, as a girl, want to date you?
- What kind of future plans do you make?
- What career paths are open to you?
- As you think about the differences, what about your life today would be changed, if anything?
- What plans and opportunities would be different for you?
- As you walk in the other gender's shoes, high heels, loafers, or whatever, in what way(s) would you see changes in your new life?

If you were the other, you would be confronted with demands, obligations and expectations that you have not had to consider before. It might feel enormously complicated and overwhelming or maybe a whole lot simpler. What is the impact on you?

As you imagine being the other, can you feel the stresses that you wouldn't want to deal with? Perhaps that tells us more about gender differences than anything else we can say.

Take some time to look over your notes on your gender switch. This is a great place to stop and share your insights with a friend or mate and discuss what would have been different. What kind of things came up for you?

The kinds of things you have included in your list spell out the major differences in gender communication, opportunities and lifestyle.

To say there are only men and women in the world is to

deny the amazing variety of men among men and women among women. This is not about sexual orientation. It is about how we live our gender identification.

This is manifested in dress, hobbies, size, strength, choices of activities, behavior, in the way we decorate our surroundings at home, and in our work and play environment and the way we see our world. There are women who are ultra feminine and there are men who are super masculine. There are men and women who are more androgynous and people everywhere in-between.

Dave Barry's Complete Guide to Guys gives us a laugh about the differences in our communication and thinking style, but also gives us an opportunity not to take those differences so seriously. Differences can be fun, not just frustrating.

There are many other books dedicated to gender differences. Some of these are listed in the back of this book under resources.

Why does an understanding of gender differences contribute to togetherness that works? Perhaps it helps us to appreciate and accept people as they are. It also frees us from requiring the impossible—that they be like us! We need finally to understand the differences and respect and appreciate them without judging in order to successfully create togetherness that works. We are different. We are okay—*as is*.

How is it that women can just sit there and BE? (Rory 29)

> I learned that men actually do mean well by the things that
> they do and it's the only way that they understand how to
> express the way they feel. It helps me to understand the things
> my boyfriend does for me. (Gwen, 22)

Sex differences are interesting to me because I think many
times we try to relate to the opposite sex identically to the way
we relate to our own sex. If we are not aware of our differences
we get very frustrated with differing actions and responses
because they are not the same as our own way of dealing with
a situation. (Kelsie, 27)

> It is so classic to tell a man that there is something wrong,
> like, say your car is broken, and all he wants to do is fix it. Tell
> a woman your car is broken and chances are she will console
> you. (Orlie, 20)

I have learned that the masculine self is defined so much by
doing while the feminine self is defined by being. Hopefully, the
next time that I am placed in the situation where my girlfriend
says that she just wants to be with me, I will shut my mouth
about going out and doing something and try to understand
that this is what she needs. Also, when I am hurting I will be
able to explain to her that in order for me to talk about it I have
to be doing something or I will feel extremely uncomfortable
with the situation. (Israel, 19)

> When I was young, I did not see my father as having much
> respect for my mother. Most of my life I have been trying to
> convince "others" and myself that men and women are the
> same, that we basically have the same needs and desires.
> The reason I invested so much energy into proving that men
> and women are the same is that I wanted to feel okay about

being female. I wanted to be as respected and as valuable as a man. If men and women are the same, that makes me just as valuable and worthy as anybody else, including men. (Katy, 38)

When we were asked to try to experience the life of the other gender group, that really made me think about the effects a guy can have on a girl. We should care more. I have a sister and have seen what a guy can do. So I think it really hit home that women should be treated with respect and loyalty. (Aidan, 21)

Is there a way that you can explain your feelings to men so that they would understand and not be intimidated? (Gwen, 22)

I've always rebelled against the male/female role models of my 1950s parents where the woman has no life outside the home, no credit, no financial freedom, etc., etc. I was attracted to the unisex concept of the 60s that all people should be as androgynous as possible. I think I have a lot of gay friends for this reason. They have a better blending of the male/female components in their personalities, activities and lifestyles. The rules seem less rigid for them and I admire the boundary crossing freedom. So, now I accept the fact that men relate differently. My expectations are relaxed. I appreciate men by simply accepting the fact that they are from another planet, instead of stubbornly insisting that they come down to earth. This reminds me of a funny line from the movie *City Slickers* where Billy Crystal tells his buddies: "Women need a reason to have sex. Men just need a place." Ha. Ha! (Tess, 36)

"There are men and women who make the world
better just by being the kind of people they are."

—John William Gardner

I really think you should say "I do" not "I'll give it a try."

Chapter 19

The Best Age to Get Married

"Marriage is our last, best chance to grow up."

—Joseph Barth

When people ask "what is the best age to get married, they seem to expect a magical numerical answer. Is it a chronological age that we reach or do we have some lessons to learn to reach relational maturity before we tie the knot?

A group of young college women asked "What is the best age to get married, the age with the best chances of success? Is it different for men and women?" The answers to their questions formed this chapter.

Simply put, the best time to get married is when you know yourself quite well and have chosen someone special with whom you want to live the rest of your life. I translate *best time* as meaning when having a successful lasting relationship that enhances both of you is most likely.

The *best time* question is not simple because it's not about a magic number or age. It's about relational maturity.

That relational maturity includes Physical, Emotional, Social, Psychological, Financial and Spiritual elements.

Physically, perhaps the best time to get married is during the teens and early twenties because the body is easily aroused, sex is very much in the forefront of each other's minds, and a young female can handle the physical demands of birthing babies with relative ease. While the male is at the height of his sexual prowess between eighteen and twenty, as he ages, he becomes better able to meet his partners' needs as well as his own.

However, getting along with a marriage partner, other than sexually, and parenting children, making decisions about life and finances, and planning for the future are skills that are rarely developed with this age group. So overall, adolescence isn't the best time to get married! An age where there is greater personal maturity is probably better.

Emotionally, couples need to have self-control and be able to respect their partner even when having a mood swing or a tough day. When a person lashes out at their partner or mate verbally or physically, emotional closeness will be damaged and distancing will occur.

The respect for togetherness requires there be no game playing with the other's emotions. Constantly questioning the partner or being verbally unkind erodes closeness even when followed by an apology.

Psychologically, couples are better prepared for marriage after having experienced some wins and losses of their own, separately. After all, life is full of ups and downs. Also, it helps if they have tried on different behaviors and selected some that work for them long-range. They are ready to be together with someone when they know how to be alone.

Mature people are aware of their feelings and have access to them in appropriate ways as part of their development. They are trustworthy and can determine if someone they are attracted to is also trustworthy. They can say they are wrong when they're wrong and request forgiveness. They can resolve conflict before going to sleep at night, or at least try.

They can list, in a rational way, what they're looking for in a mate in order to be selective about a person to share their life with. In short, they choose their friends and dates by design instead of by default or on the basis of a wild weekend. They are capable of wrestling with the issue of how much *you, me,* and *we* in order to keep themselves intact along with the relationship. They have grown up, literally.

Socially, grown-up people are ready to deal with two families and the complications of their mate's family baggage as well as their strengths and talents. They know how to be in the world with other people without relying on drugs or alcohol or embarrassing the person they are with. They can be with their mate and enhance the social situation. They are able to speak up and communicate their needs and wants and opinions as well as be a good listener and allow other people to express their points of view.

Financially, both persons considering marrying should come to grips with the realities of money and have personal self-control over credit cards and impulsive spending. Some kind of financial plan needs to be in place before the couple marries in order to cover the daily living expenses and to plan for the unexpected. At the very least, in order to have a steady income, employment needs to be a part of the picture. Along with a savings strategy, a long-term goal of planning for a family and retirement needs to be part of the conversation.

Spiritually, we all need to discover some kind of meaning beyond today's events. What gifts do we have to share in the world and what purpose do we have for being here? How can this relationship deepen that purpose and expand what I am here for? How can I help the other person be more of who they are? Can I give up self-centeredness and focus on the *you* and the *we* as well as the *me*?

And that's not all . . .

Planning for the possibility of children requires more of each of these categories. The strain and stress as well as the joy of the wee little one will complicate any relationship big time as well as require great maturity on the part of the parents. You might want to practice with a puppy!

As you can imagine, the age at which a person gains clarity regarding these issues might be different for each person. Males and females might have different priorities. Age twenty-eight sounds good, but for some, it may be thirty-eight or older before these maturity hurdles are met. For others, mid-twenties might be right.

ACTION ITEM ·········▶

Choice Choices

Let me ask you a question. Have you changed your thinking in the last five years? Do you have different tastes in activities, clothes, goals, attitudes and perhaps friends than you did five years ago?

I raise the question because the person you will be five years from now will have to live with the choices you make today. That is, the person you will become will be hostage to the health choices, friendship choices and your choice of a mate. Can you live with your choices? Do you have any recurring doubts?

Red and green flags to consider

So we have looked at the categories of relational maturity. Let us now ask some questions about the person(s) you are considering for marriage or partnership. Write down your answers and any comments you care to make.

Physically
- Are you attracted to him/her?
- Do they share similar attitudes towards health (i.e. fitness, diet, hygiene) to you?

- Do you enjoy doing things with them? Do you have interests in common?
- Do you feel safe with them sexually?

Emotionally
- Can you count on them to have their emotions under control?
- Do they play with or take advantage of your emotions?
- Are you always on guard with them?
- Can you trust your deep feelings with them?

Psychologically
- Do you consider them to have their act together?
- Do you question their impulsivity?
- Have they grown up to the point where they are able to share *your* life?

Socially
- Do you have things in common that you like to do?
- Do you ever find yourself apologizing for their behavior to your friends?
- Does their lifestyle work for them in a positive way? Would it work for you?

Financially
- Do they have a financial plan that includes savings?
- Do they value and share your attitude towards money?
- Can you trust them with money? Your money?
- Are they burdened with debt?
- Do they demand extravagances from you when you have a "cautious" budget? (Or the other way around?)
- Do they respect your attitude towards money?

Spiritually
- Do they share your spiritual beliefs?
- Do they live their lives according to a behavior standard

that you respect?

- If you have children, can you feel confident in sharing their beliefs in the raising of the children?
- Are they trustworthy and do you trust them? And vice versa!

These questions are designed to help you think through your understanding of your potential partner. If some of the questions raise red flags for you or if you cannot comfortably answer them, it is time to have some serious conversations with your special other. If you cannot talk about these things with them, then that by itself may be a red flag about your readiness to get married. If on the other hand, you comfortably answer the questions, there is a green light to go ahead, if you choose to.

Relational maturity may be the final developmental task. Many people skip the maturity and practice on a first or second marriage instead of growing themselves first. If a person really wants a successful and lasting first marriage, I recommend doing the work of becoming the special person you are first, before selecting that special other.

When you reach 90 percent of all these six goals, I say, go for it! Asking this question "When is the best age for me to get married?" in the first place shows maturity.

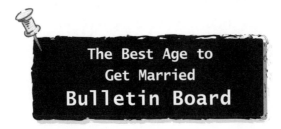

The Best Age to Get Married
Bulletin Board

I am tied to him, attached forever through a bad and brief relationship and a good son. I have not seen or spoken to him in 19 years. He will always be on my map. (Eliza, 49)

I did not fall in love immediately this time. It was a gradual growth. First we became friends, sharing past experiences, learning each other's likes and dislikes, hopes and dreams, and discovering we were very much alike. With this solid foundation paved, we began to build a relationship based on mutual caring, understanding and love. (Ellie, 44)

When my husband and I got married, I just assumed we would figure it out. There are issues in our marriage that I do not understand. I thought that we had problems and that we needed to see a counselor; however, I have discovered that we are simply in a profound relationship that takes a great deal of effort to maintain. I have learned that I have taken things for granted in some aspects. I have learned that marriage is the hardest thing I have ever done, yet the most fulfilling. (Lauren, 34)

Twenty-three is the best age because you know the person forever by then. (Cam, 10)

I had no idea how much my life would change when I got married. While it is a lot of work sometimes, there is more joy than I could have imagined. I no longer feel alone. (Carol, 27)

After reading this and thinking about the questions, I'm afraid I'm not as ready to get married as I thought. This makes me sad because my boyfriend is so wonderful and cute. But I guess we are just too young. (Martha, 18)

My girlfriend borrowed my credit card, charged a bunch of stuff and then dumped me. I'm stuck with major bills. Boy did I choose the wrong girl. (Bill, 29)

The beauty of our second marriage is that we are old enough to know who we are and we're old enough and smart enough to know what a blessing it is to fall in love with your best friend. (Ellen, 58)

292

But, Mom, I had to fly home.
I need somebody on my side.

Chapter 20

Families: What Works, What Hurts

"What can you do to promote world peace? Go home and love your family."

— Mother Teresa

The family is the cocoon where we learn the art of relationships. Take all the lessons of this book, and practice them in the environment you call home and with the people you call family.

The family, it seems, can be a source of great safety and growth or a place of great pain and suffering. What a wonderful experience it is to be a member of a supportive family where there is the presence of warmth, love, caring, consideration and a sense of place for each person. To feel that parents enjoy their role and desire growth for each member of the family is to feel safety.

What a sad experience it is to feel unsafe, unwanted and uncared for in a setting which is called family but which is a source of abuse, anger and hurt.

Time spent in the first family creates memories to be retained and cherished. Time spent in the second family mentioned is to be resented, forgotten and buried.

Different family experiences give us different models for us to follow as we create new families. One is to be duplicated as a positive model. Many times, the other is duplicated by default if the members do not have the opportunity to unlearn the negative. The abuse cycle can be multi-generational. This is why learning how to create togetherness that works is so essential for healthy families. Alex Haley put it this way: "In every conceivable manner, the family is link to our past, bridge to our future."

A neutral feeling about this first network of people in our lives doesn't seem possible. It certainly doesn't happen often.

Confucius said, "To put the world right in order, we must first put the nation in order; to put the nation in order, we must first put the family in order; to put the family in order, we must first cultivate our personal life; we must first set our hearts right."

ACTION ITEM ·········➤

Questions about Family

  ▶ What feeling do you have about your family?
  ▶ What family experiences do you want to recreate?
  ▶ What memories do you want to forget or replace?
Write down your answers in your journal.

Feelings about the family can differ from sibling to sibling.

One child might say that the family was a safe and supportive place to live. Another sibling labels it dysfunctional and denounces the experiences there. The absence of a nurturing family can impact the stability of a person for their whole life. Many people long for a family other than the one they have, with the belief that the grass is always greener somewhere else. Many others cherish the warmth of their family memories and grieve deeply for what they had once parents are gone and the family unit is no more.

There is no more powerful setting that impacts a child's life than the family the child grows up in.

All in the Same Family?

As alluded to, in a family of siblings, we tend to think we're all growing up in the same environment. Yet, no two children grow up in exactly the same family. Family dynamics change with each child and with passing time.

We have a tendency to say, "My sister and I grew up in the same family, so why are we so different?" The truth is, you didn't grow up in the same family! Over time, the family goes through change and metamorphosis and emerges not the same family as before.

If, for example, we grow up as a first-born child, the parents are fresh to the parenting experience with us. The first child becomes a little adult because, after all, the first-born lives with adults, and mimics what they see.

As the first-born, the child is the focus of attention and the recipient of the parents' early efforts, learning and mistakes. There is energetic attention and support. The traditional family may have a mother, father, and the first-born child. Other family configurations of single parents or same sex parents or stepparents can also provide the environment in which a first child is nurtured.

If a sister or brother is added to the family system, this new child grows up where there are three adults—Mother, Father, the adult-like child—all taking care of the second born.

In addition to enjoying the new child, the first born may have mixed feelings about the second born because the child is smaller, cuter, and is now getting all the attention. The first-born may be resentful, because where before the spotlight was on them, they now have to share. They might also be protectors of the newborn and advocates for them with the parents and other people.

As they grow, the older sibling might protect the younger in school and then bully them at home. They can be conflicted about their feelings for this new companion and for the competition for attention. No matter what, they have bonded as siblings. Parents have the task of teaching them to get along. Perhaps a third child is born, and this new child grows up into yet a different family system. Now the former youngest has lost their position and becomes a middle child. The family dynamics have changed. The two existing children have to change, too.

ACTION ITEM ⋯⋯⋯⋯⋯➤

More Family Questions
- ▶ What birth order did you hold in your family?
- ▶ What were the advantages of your position in the family (oldest, youngest, middle)?
- ▶ What were the disadvantages?
- ▶ How were you affected by the changes in your family?

Write these insights down in your journal.

The energetic, positive, career starting, twenty-five-year-old parents are a very different set of parents from an older couple of, say, forty. If nothing else, the older parents at least tire sooner! They also have the benefit of greater life experience.

Therefore, when we say we grew up in the same family, it's really not true because with each additional child and at each developmental stage, the evolving interpersonal dynamics changed everything. Our parents aren't the same because having children is changing them. Maybe there was also a job change, or divorce, or financial changes, or a stepparent is now involved.

If these things happen, the experience of parenting is very different than the first time around. The children are the recipients of all this change and they take it all in, trying to understand how they fit with the newness. It has become a different family system.

Sometimes people aren't treated the same as they were

before. In a blended family, for example, a first-born child may suddenly become a middle child if the stepparent has older children. That changes things. Children may feel that the stepparent favors their own children over them. Research shows that step parenting is tough to do and that blended families face divorce frequently not because of the relationship between the spouses, but because of parenting conflicts.

ACTION ITEM ··········▶

What Is Your Place?

If you're part of a blended family, how did that change affect your "place" in the family? Write these insights in your journal.

Grandparents are raising many more children today than ever before. Step-parenting is common. Single parents take on the tasks of both parents and tire under the demands. Same sex parents are raising children in a newly defined family. Children raised in the foster care system have an extended family of other children like themselves. Adopted children are chosen to be part of an instant family. More and more couples are adopting orphans from other countries and taking on the challenges of being multiracial/multicultural families.

The family is changing but whatever form it takes, it will always be the strongest force in a child's life.

ACTION ITEM ··········▶

Describing Your Family
  ▶ Describe your family of origin.
  ▶ Describe your family today.
  ▶ Who are the members and what roles do they play?

Singles develop friendships that become family to them. An adopted family can provide a place of holding, healing, renewal, love, and the nurturing each of us needs to function in today's world. This family they choose.

In some cases, young people leave a family in the hopes of finding a new and different family experience with someone else. Adopting a new or different family of friends may nurture them differently from their family of origin.

While the ideal is for a family to remain intact, divorce is more common than we would wish for in our culture. A parent may divorce their mate and also choose to leave their family to find a more nourishing environment for themselves. By moving away, they may join others or remarry to create a new family unit that they hope will be healing for them.

In so doing, they leave behind the other parent and the children to deal with a difficult adjustment. The family left behind will feel the loss for the rest of their lives. Extended family members (grandparents, aunts, uncles, cousins, close friends) can add nurturing to a family that is adjusting to a break up.

George Burns, the comedian quipped that "happiness is having a large, loving, caring, close knit family...in another city." In his humor, he acknowledged that some families are not poster children for closeness.

The Family Goal

A healthy family that thrives can provide a cocoon where the learning experiences of this book can happen and the members of that family unit feel safe.

The experiences and needs of holding, connecting, belonging and attaching to others can occur in the environment where family members receive support and love.

The family therapist Virginia Satir pointed out, "Feelings of worth can flourish only in an atmosphere where individual differences are appreciated, mistakes are tolerated, communication is open, and rules are flexible—the kind of atmosphere that is found in a nurturing family."

Additionally, Eda Leshan tells us, "Becoming responsible adults is not a matter of whether children hang up their pajamas or put dirty towels in the hamper, but whether they care about themselves and others—and whether they see everyday chores as related to how we treat this planet."

We have much to teach our children that impact not only their lives, but also how they will interact with others.

The Dinner Table

One of the key places for families to connect and to feel nurtured is at the daily dinner table if active conversation and interaction are encouraged. Surveys show that teens who shared family meals five or more times a week are less likely to use drugs and that they do better in school and feel better about themselves.

For many, dinner can be a time of stress and anxiety instead of fun and sharing or it may be nonexistent as members separately grab fast food or schedule themselves to be otherwise occupied. It surprises me how many people report never sitting down to supper/dinner together as a family.

Dinner time was a daily ritual in my family for which I was grateful. The meal began with the blessing and giving thanks. The food may not have been fancy but it was always prepared lovingly. It was a time when we shared what had happened during the day and planned for the next day. It was about family togetherness.

For holidays, the extended family was always together and, after the meal, we remained at the table where we shared jokes and news and wisecracks—sometimes for hours.

When members of the family feel listened to and heard, they feel valued and therefore value themselves.

Mealtime Memoir
  ▶ What was dinnertime like for you as a child?
  ▶ Did it change when you were a teenager?
  ▶ What is dinnertime like for you now?

If you are looking for more meaningful conversation at dinner time than "What's new? Nothing." Or "How was your day? Fine," consider a product called "Food for Talk".

"Food for Talk" is a box of cards with quotations or conversation starters that are interesting and fun. Selecting one and then having each person respond with their ideas or experiences gives a great jump-start to real expressions of thoughts and feelings. All of us love the attention that comes when we are an active part of a lively conversation. The cards also contribute to lively dinner party conversation. Check out www.foodfortalk.net.

300

Families that do not have the dinnertime ritual of checking in and talking to each other about the day miss the opportunity to grow together. When parents say that they are losing touch with their kids, the first place to correct the problem is to share meals, even if it is "take out" or "bring in" food.

A prescription for improved family health is to focus on the expectation that dinner is a priority time that provides food and also food for thought. It is a ritual deeply needed today by all of us.

Need help getting started?

Turning off the TV is a first step to better communication and digestion! Giving everyone a chance to speak and share is another step to togetherness.

When it is safe to express an opinion, children learn how to trust themselves as well as others. Love expressed in these interactions becomes not a concept but an everyday happening. Family members tend each other by listening, and the richness of togetherness makes returning home at the end of each day something to look forward to.

The bottom line is this: We all need family.

Do you know what the word FAMILY means?

FAMILY = (F)ATHER (A)ND (M)OTHER,
(I) (L)OVE (Y)OU

E-mail, source unknown

Jane Howard put it this way. "Call it a clan, call it a network, call it a tribe, call it a family: Whatever you call it, whoever you are, you need one."

We may be blessed to be born into a healthy one, adopted into one, create it ourselves or build an extended family. We may be challenged to leave an unhealthy environment and to search for a new place or group to belong, but the courage to do that can also support the energy needed to build a new family.

The family provides a space to practice the hard work and skills of relationships. I repeat, the bottom line is, we all need family.

Family is the key place in our lives that teaches us the art of relationships and how to create the togetherness that works! Take all the lessons of this book and practice them in the environment you call home and with the people you call family.

The richness ahead will create challenges, delightful moments and memories galore for you to recall.

Togetherness is worth the work.

You deserve it.

I wish you joy.

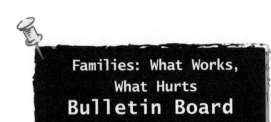
My father was a wonderful and kind man. He was consistent. He did not let me down. (Eliza, 49)

> For most of my life I have been "doing battle" with my father. As a father of two sons I am concerned whether or not I can raise them without resorting to physical violence as my father had. I must say that my consciousness has helped me stop using violence and I think my two sons are better for it. (Isaac, 47)

My sister and I like to talk about the old days at home. We experienced everything so differently and learned so much from hearing each other's stories. Almost everything is funny by the time we have looked at it from two different points of view. (Noreen, 53)

> I turned to my family recently and have learned that I am accepted, with all my faults, ideas, fears and everything. My parents are always able to see a step ahead a "better version" and I am able to trudge onward. (Noemi, 31)

One of my favorite family memories is that of sitting at the table after dinner and just talking. (Jan, 64)

"Friends are the family we choose for ourselves."

—Edna Buchanan

References for
Further Growth

Anger: The Misunderstood Emotion by Carol Tavris; Revised Edition; New York: Simon & Schuster, 1989; ISBN: 0671675230

Best Friends: The Pleasures and Perils of Girls' and Women's Friendships by Terri Apter and Ruthellen Josselson; New York: Crown Publishers, 1998; ISBN: 0609601164

Crossing the Unknown Sea: Work as a Pilgrimage of Identity by David Whyte; New York: Riverhead Books, 2001; ISBN: 1573221783

Families by Jane Howard; New Brunswick, N.J.: Transaction Publishers, 1999; ISBN: 0765804689

Getting the Love You Want: A Guide for Couples by Harville Hendrix; 1st Owl books ed.; New York: H. Holt and Co., 2001; ISBN: 0805068953

Getting to 'I Do': The Secret to Doing Relationships Right by Dr. Pat Allen and Sandra Harmon; New York : W. Morrow & Co., Feb 1995; ISBN: 0380718154 (paperback) 0688112986 (hardback)

Going the Distance: Secrets to Lifelong Loves by Lonnie G. Barbach and David L. Geisinger; New York: Doubleday, 1991; ISBN: 0685261128

Hardball for Women: Winning at the Game of Business by Pat Heim with Susan K. Golant; Revised Edition; New York: Plume, 2005; ISBN: 0452286417

Helping Families to Change by Virginia Satir, James Stachowiak and Harvey A. Taschman; New York: J. Aronson, 1975; ISBN: 0876682387

How to Survive the Loss of Love by Melba Colgrove, Harold H. Bloomfield and Peter McWilliams; Los Angeles: Prelude Press, Nov 1993; ISBN: 0931580455 (Out-of-Print)

If the Buddha Dated: Handbook for Finding Love on a Spiritual Path by Charlotte Sophia Kasl; New York: Penguin/Arkana, 1999; ISBN: 0140195831

In A Different Voice: Psychological Theory and Women's Development by Carol Gilligan; Boston: Harvard University Press, Sept 1993; ISBN: 0674445449

John Bowlby on Human Attachment by John H. Hoover; CYC-Online March 2004 v62 online [Accessed 9/05/05] http://www.cyc-net.org/cyc-online/cycol-0304-bowlby.html

Life Launch: A Passionate Guide to the Rest of Your Life by Frederic M. Hudson and Pamela D. McLean; Santa Barbara, CA : Hudson Press; March 1995; ISBN: 1884433847

Living with Death and Dying by Elisabeth Kubler-Ross; New York: Macmillan, 1981; ISBN: 0025671403

Making Contact by Virginia Satir; Millbrae, CA: Celestial Arts, 1976; ISBN: 0890871191

Managing Transitions: Making the Most of Change by William Bridges; 2nd ed.; Cambridge, MA: Perseus Pub., 2003; ISBN: 0738208248

Moving Beyond Words by Gloria Steinem; New York: Simon & Schuster, 1994; ISBN: 0671649728

On Death and Dying by Elisabeth Kübler-Ross; New York: MacMillian; 1969

Out of the Depths: An Autobiographical Study of Mental Disorder and Religious Experience by Anton Theophilus Boisen; New York: Harper, 1960

Outrageous Acts and Everyday Rebellions by Gloria Steinem; 1st ed.; New York: Holt, Rinehart, and Winston, 1983; ISBN: 0030632366

Rebuilding: When Your Relationship Ends by Bruce Fisher, Robert Alberti; 3rd ed.; Atascadero, CA: Impact Publishers, 2000; ISBN: 188623017X

Relationship Rescue: A Seven-Step Strategy for Reconnecting with Your Partner by Philip C. McGraw; New York: Hyperion, 2000; ISBN: 0786866314

Revising Herself: The Story of Women's identity from College to Midlife by Ruthellen Josselson; San Francisco: Jossey-Bass, 1987; ISBN: 1555420494

Revolution from Within: A Book of Self-Esteem by Gloria Steinem; Boston: Little Brown & Co., Jan 1993; ISBN: 0316812471

Satir Step-by-Step: A Guide to Creating Change in Families by Virginia Satir and Michele Baldwin; Palo Alto, CA: Science and Behavior Books, 1983; ISBN: 0831400684

Sex, Time, and Power: How Women's Sexuality Shaped Human Evolution by Leonard Shlain; New York: Viking, 2003; ISBN: 0670032336

Talking from 9 to 5: How Women's and Men's Conversational Styles Affect Who Gets heard, Who Gets Credit, and What Gets Done at Work by Deborah Tannen; New York: W. Morrow, 1994; ISBN: 0688112439

The Adult Years: Mastering the Art of Self-Renewal by Frederic M. Hudson; San Francisco: Jossey-Bass, 1999; ISBN: 0787948012

The Alphabet versus the Goddess: The Conflict between Word and Image by Leonard Shlain; New York: Viking, 1998; ISBN: 0670878839

The Five Love Languages: How to Express Heartfelt Commitment to Your Mate by Gary Chapman; Waterville, Me.: Thorndike Press, 2005; ISBN: 078627459X (hardbound) & 1594150818 (paperback)

The Heart Aroused: Poetry and the Preservation of the Soul in Corporate America by David Whyte; New York: Currency Doubleday, 1994; ISBN: 0385423500

The House of Belonging by David Whyte; Langley, WA: Many Rivers Press, 1997; ISBN: 0962152439

The Knight in Rusty Armor by Robert Fisher; Chatsworth, CA: Wilshire Book Co., May 1989; ISBN: 0879804211

The Little Prince by Antoine de Saint-Exupéry; translated from the French by Katherine Woods; San Diego: Harcourt Brace; Oct 1982; ISBN: 0156465116

The Princess Who Believed in Fairy Tales: A Story for Modern Times by Marcia Grad; North Hollywood, CA: Wilshire Book Co., May 1995; ISBN: 087980436X

The Relationship Rescue Workbook: Exercises and Self-tests to Help You Reconnect with Your Partner by Philip C. McGraw; New York: Hyperion, 2000; ISBN: 0786886048

The Road Less Traveled: A New Psychology of Love, Traditional Values and Spiritual Growth by M. Scott Peck, MD; 25th Anniversary edition; New York: Simon & Schuster, 2002; ISBN: 0743238257

The Space Between Us: Exploring the Dimension of Human Relationships by Ruthellen Josselson; San Francisco: Jossey-Bass, 1992; ISBN: 1555424104

The Velveteen Rabbit by Margery Williams, illustrations by William Nicholson; Deerfield Beach, FL: Health Communications, 2005; ISBN: 0757303331

Things will be Different for My Daughter: A Practical Guide to Building Her Self- Esteem and Self-Reliance by Mindy Bingham and Sandy Stryker with Susan Allstetter Neufeldt, Ph.D.; New York: Penguin USA; Feb 1995; ISBN: 0140241256

Tuesdays with Morrie: An Old Man, A Young Man, and Life's Greatest Lesson by Mitch Albon; New York: Doubleday; 1997; ISBN: 0385484518

What Color Is Your Parachute? by Richard Nelson Bolles; Berkeley, CA: Ten Speed Press, 1971; ISSN: 8755-4658

You Just Don't Understand: Women and Men in Conversation by Deborah Tannen; New York: Morrow, 1990; ISBN: 0688078222

Your Many Faces by Virginia Satir; Millbrae, CA: Celestial Arts, 1978; ISBN: 0890871876 (Hardback) 0890871205 (Paperback)

Mapping Your Relationships
Sample Maps and Symbols Key

Use these symbols to identify parts of your map. This is a review of the directions you have read in each chapter.

⭘	Individual in your life of importance to you
⭕ (dashed)	Individual who is deceased or not personally known to you (mentor/hero)
◉ (group circle)	Group or team
Holding **H**	Those who really held you
Holding **h**	Those who you held
Attachment **A**	Those with whom you have an attachment
Validation **V**	Those who were/are nutritious and validating to you
Mirroring **MP**	Those who have mirrored you in a positive way
Sexual Relationship **SR**	Those with whom you have had a sexual relationship
Trustworthy **T**	Those who have demonstrated that they are trustworthy
Mentor **M**	Those who served you as mentor or hero
Rules **R**	People/Groups who set the Rules for you
Togetherness **F**	Close or intimate friend
Love ❤ **L**	Those you decided to love and who have decided to love you
Tending **RT**	Those from whom you received tending
Tending **GT**	Those you have given tending

Sample relationship maps at different ages

Juanita, age 5 — kindergarten

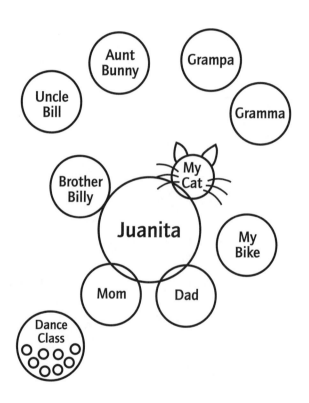

Juanita, age 10 – 5th grade

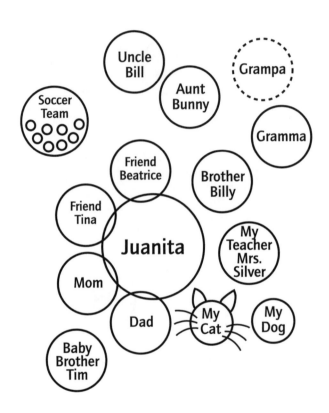

310

Juanita, age 15 — sophmore

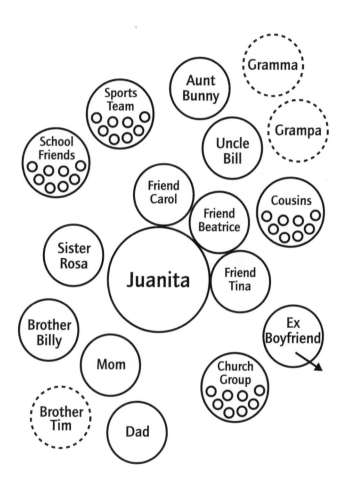

Juanita, age 20

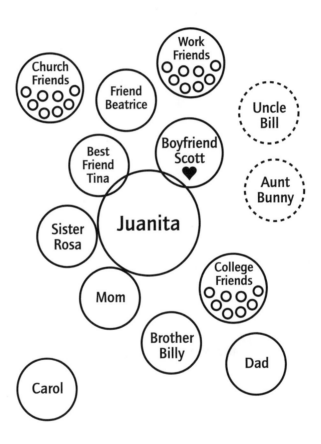

Acknowledgments and Appreciations

With grateful appreciation to the encouragers and believers in this project without whom the book would not have happened.

Margi Murray, my student and my teacher. Thanks for living the learnings and believing this book should be written to the point that you were willing to commit time and yourself to do some serious nudging.

Allen Loman, cartoonist, for drawing the humor into this quite serious book.

Gail M. Kearns, To Press and Beyond, for pushing and prodding as my editor and book shepherd to make this work fit for publication.

All of my students who asked the hard questions and participated in finding the answers.

Peri Poloni of Knockout design, for the thoughtful and artistic process of cover design.

Chris Nolt of Cirrus Design, for creating the book layout and managing frequent smiles and laughter while dealing with incredible details.

Ruthellen Josselson for *the Space Between Us*, the launching pad of the Human Relationships class that I taught and learned from.

Mindy Bingham who years ago encouraged me to write the book and for her availability to answer tons of questions.

Dan Poynter for making sure I didn't die with this book inside me.

Claire Elkins for inviting me to speak to her college health classes and coaxing each chapter out of me with good questions.

Bonnie Stephenson, researcher and librarian extraordinaire who always had time for one more question.

My relationships, the goods ones, the bad ones and even the ugly ones, because each of them have taught me important lessons.

Manuscript reviewers: Claire Elkins, Barbara Goutierre, Frances Bolles Haynes, Holland Carney, Vivian Clecak, Carrie Lynn Moore, Sue Bottassi, Pam Shepherd, Roe Picolli, Mindy Bingham, Dr. Pat Allen, Dr. M.P. Wylie, Dr. Melina Friedman, Lydia Pettis, Genia Pickett. Thanks for your patience in plowing through the pages and for your suggestions to make this better.

Laurie Pick who transcribed all my lectures into word documents.

Genia Pickett for living the relationship that matters.

And while she is not here to read this, my mother, who taught me about relationships, loving and life.